THE
LEADERSHIP
STAR

THE
LEADERSHIP
STAR

A PRACTICAL GUIDE TO
BUILDING ENGAGEMENT

BRIAN HARTZER

WILEY

First published in 2021 by John Wiley & Sons Australia, Ltd
42 McDougall St, Milton Qld 4064
Office also in Melbourne

Typeset in Chaparral Pro 11pt/14pt

© John Wiley & Sons Australia, Ltd 2021

The moral rights of the author have been asserted

ISBN: 978-0-730-39083-1

A catalogue record for this book is available from the National Library of Australia

Cover design and images by Wiley

Printed in Singapore by Markono Print Media Pte Ltd

SKYA8B510CC-8665-4649-BD87-B36293684ECA_031721

Disclaimer
The material in this publication is of the nature of general comment only, and does not represent professional advice. It is not intended to provide specific guidance for particular circumstances and it should not be relied on as the basis for any decision to take action or not take action on any matter which it covers. Readers should obtain professional advice where appropriate, before making any such decision. To the maximum extent permitted by law, the author and publisher disclaim all responsibility and liability to any person, arising directly or indirectly from any person taking or not taking action based on the information in this publication.

For Jim Hartzer

Who, through the way he lived his life,

taught me all the important lessons in this book —

even though it took me 30 years to realise it.

CONTENTS

ACKNOWLEDGEMENTS

This book would not have been possible without inspiration and assistance from a number of people who have helped me develop these concepts over the past two decades.

I have been blessed to work with and learn from many talented executives over the years — all of whom have contributed in important ways to the making of this book.

In my ANZ days, Damian Cotchett, Fiona Ryan, Miriam Silva, Barbara Wilby, Peter Hawkins, Sonya Clancy, Louis Hawke, John Harries, Greg Camm, John Connolly and John McFarlane all taught me important lessons about leadership. More recently I have been fortunate to learn from inspirational CEOs such as Stephen Hester, Ross McEwen, Gail Kelly, David Morgan, Bob Joss, Alan Joyce, Sir Ralph Norris and Jamie Dimon.

While the Leadership Star framework in this book predates my time at Westpac, I am grateful for the enthusiastic contributions and support from Westpac's Human Resources and Communications teams.

In writing the book, I am particularly grateful to Marj Lefroy — who first encouraged me to write this book more than a decade ago and contributed some early drafting.

I would also like to thank Satyendra Chelvendra (Chelvi), Carl Sparks, Tim Ford, Barbara Wilby, Joel Pearce, Carolyn Hartzer Pearce, Stephen Hester, Bob Joss, Sir Ralph Norris, Ryan Stokes, Craig Tapper and

Maurizio Floris, who all read drafts, shared insights, ideas and stories, and whose feedback was invaluable in helping me sort out my thinking. This book is immensely better for their generosity in sharing their wisdom and experience with me.

I'd also like to thank Jeanne Ryckmans, Allison Hiew, Lucy Raymond, Chris Shorten and the whole team at John Wiley & Sons for helping turn my initial manuscript into a fully fledged book that will hopefully benefit future leaders.

Finally, I'd like to thank my amazing wife, Georgy, and our wonderful children for their continued love, support and confidence in me over the past — challenging — 12 months.

PREFACE

This book is designed to help leaders at all levels — from newly minted team leaders to established CEOs — to build and sustain highly engaged teams.

It presents a five-point framework that I call the 'Leadership Star' — a visual memory device I created to help me recall and apply engagement lessons that I'd learned through trial and error and from watching great leaders in action. As a self-taught leader — I don't have an MBA — these lessons were collected over a 30-year career in banking that spanned roles on four continents and culminated in my time as CEO of Westpac from 2015 to 2019.

While my experience has predominantly (though not exclusively) been in a commercial, financial services setting, feedback from other leaders with whom I've shared these lessons convinces me that they apply equally to government, academic, community and not-for-profit organisations as well.

Although many of the stories in this book are drawn from my time at ANZ, Royal Bank of Scotland and Westpac, this is not a book about those companies or my time as CEO of Westpac.

Because of the circumstances of my departure from Westpac — which I touch on briefly at the end of this book — I am conscious that some people may dismiss what I have to say, or seek to highlight differences between the lessons in this book and what they see as my failings as a CEO.

While I am all too aware of my weaknesses, the experience of other leaders who have applied the Leadership Star convinces me that the model works. My hope is that, by sharing the lessons in this book, other leaders and their employees will benefit from the good bits and avoid some of the mistakes that I made along the way.

I've subtitled this book 'A practical guide to building engagement' because it reflects my and other leaders' actual experience in applying this framework to our daily work lives. While this book contains many specific ideas and suggestions, the good news is you don't need an MBA to understand it or get started. It's designed to be simple enough that you can carry the five points around in your head, while being nuanced enough to help you diagnose and take action on things that may be holding your team or business back.

So whether you're new to the challenge of leadership, an experienced leader, or an established CEO who needs a structure against which you can assess your current approach, this book is for you.

Brian Hartzer
Sydney, October 2020

INTRODUCTION

'But what do I *personally* need to do?'

There was a long pause, and the two human resources experts on the other side of the table stared back at me, blankly.

We had just finished reviewing the latest results of the annual staff satisfaction survey for my business. The results were okay, but not great.

It was a typical survey: staff had been asked to rank on a scale of 1–10 their response to statements such as 'I enjoy my job', 'My manager recognises me for the work that I do' and 'I rarely think about leaving'.

The HR team had just finished presenting the results, organised in themes such as 'communications', 'staff recognition', 'training', 'manager quality' and so on.

Some areas had improved, most had stayed the same and a couple had declined.

But there was little in the way of practical suggestions about what we as a business leadership team could do to improve the results — let alone where I as the head of the business could intervene to improve things.

Hence my question — and the HR team didn't have any good answers.

This was frustrating because, three years into my role managing the credit card business of a large Australian bank, I was convinced that a strong culture and high staff satisfaction were critical to building a high-performing business.

Although I was relatively new to leading a business, having spent the first ten years of my career as a management consultant, it seemed obvious that a strong culture was important. There were few true credit card experts in our market, and I reasoned that if the best people in our industry wanted to work with us then we would have a sustainable advantage over our competitors.

Taking action to increase what we now call 'staff engagement' was therefore a critical business priority.

The Human Resources team and the engagement consultants that we used provided broad-based programs to address many of the specific issues raised in the surveys. We studied the verbatim feedback and held facilitated sessions to understand what the comments meant in practice. Managers talked to their people about engagement and completed 'action sheets' that documented their priority areas for improvement and allowed us to track progress. We created 'Action Teams' of motivated staff from all levels to develop solutions to many of the issues that were raised and empowered them to get on and fix things. They implemented a number of innovative ideas that worked well.

Over time survey scores improved. But it never felt like I was doing enough. I wasn't prepared to delegate such an important issue purely to the Human Resources team. I wanted to know: what do I *personally* need to do as the leader to improve engagement?

The quest to answer that question became an ongoing focus of my professional life over the two decades that followed—through senior roles in three separate banks, overseeing businesses that spanned three continents and multiple countries.

In this book, I want to share what I've learned.

Why engagement?

If you're reading this book, there's a fair chance that you already accept the premise that building a highly engaged workforce is critical to business performance.

There are a variety of ways of measuring engagement, although the organisations I've worked for have each used some variant of either the Aon Hewitt 'Say, Stay, and Strive' model or the Gallup 12-point survey[1] to provide a comparable benchmark across companies.

Whichever measure your company uses, engagement is a significant step up on staff satisfaction. Beyond the question of 'How satisfied are you at work?', it measures the extent to which an employee is *psychologically committed to the organisation* and the work that they are doing.

Do employees understand what the organisation is about? Do they like the people they work with? Are they proud to work there? Are they committed to putting in that extra effort needed to achieve great results? Do they believe the company has their interests at heart? Do they think their manager is good? Do they believe the company is ethical?

Said another way, an engagement score is shorthand for how employees feel about their workplace. It boils down a number of issues into an overall measure of emotional commitment that allows comparisons both within and across companies and team leaders.

Engagement surveys assess this by asking employees about the extent to which they:

- would recommend the organisation to others

- intend to stay or leave in the near future

- feel challenged and rewarded by their managers

- have the right training and support

- see opportunities to advance their career

- have friends at work

- are proud of the company and its reputation.

Responses to questions such as these are combined to generate an engagement score for the organisation overall, as well as more granular

---

[1] See aonhumancapital.com.au, 'Employee engagement' or gallup.com, 'Engage your employees to see high performance and innovation' for more information.

scores at different levels in the organisation. To ensure validity, these responses — and any verbatim comments — are kept confidential in order to encourage honesty and transparency, and companies are discouraged from linking engagement results directly to pay or promotion outcomes in ways that might unduly bias the results.

Statistical research[2] demonstrates that businesses with high staff engagement tend to see:

- higher profitability
- higher productivity
- higher customer satisfaction
- better product quality
- lower staff turnover and absenteeism
- fewer safety incidents.

These improvements create real value for an organisation's shareholders, customers and employees.

Shareholders benefit from improved profitability and reduced risk: higher, more sustainable earnings translate into a more valuable company.

Customers benefit from better product and service quality over time. You've probably had the experience of trying to get the attention of a disinterested waiter in a café, been talked down to by a dismissive call centre operator, or had to recall a tradesman after a failed attempt to fix a broken internet connection or leaking car engine. In a highly engaged organisation, the goal of delivering great products and services sees employees strive to make every customer interaction memorably great.

For employees, high engagement brings a sense of purpose, meaning, pride, personal growth and fun to their work that leads to a deeper satisfaction with their life in general. This deeper satisfaction inevitably benefits their physical and mental health, the quality of their family life, their friendships and their engagement with the broader community.

---

[2] As an example of this research, see gallup.com, 'How employee engagement drives growth'.

The limits of engagement

Admittedly, debate exists about whether high engagement *causes* high performance, or whether high-performing companies simply inspire high engagement as a result of their success. There are certainly examples of the latter, and business history is also littered with cases where a seemingly high-performing company had high engagement but still went off the rails. (Royal Bank of Scotland, where I worked for several years after it nearly failed in the Global Financial Crisis, is a good example.)

I'm also not suggesting that an increase in the engagement score *in itself* leads to higher performance. High engagement scores are an indicator, not a goal in themselves.

What I do believe, however, is that attracting and retaining great people, and creating a culture and working environment that allows them to achieve their potential, is much more likely to lead to success in a competitive environment.

And, as a leader, knowing that you've been able to make a positive impact on people's lives brings its own deep, personal satisfaction.

With multiple demands on your time, the challenge is to know what specifically you can do to drive high staff engagement.

And that's where this book comes in.

Do we really need another leadership book?

Over the past two decades, while leading or overseeing dozens of businesses across three continents, I've grappled with the question of what it takes to drive engagement. I've watched and learned from other leaders — some in my organisation, some outside of it — and looked for lessons that I could apply in my own role.

As part of my quest I've read many leadership books and met with multiple 'experts' in the field. And while many provided useful insights and academic theories, none of them gave me a practical framework that I could easily remember and apply in my daily life as a leader.

Over time, I gathered the insights together in a simple, five-point framework (the Leadership Star) — that I began sharing with leaders in the businesses I was running. A number of leaders who applied this framework saw tremendous improvements in engagement, as well as standout business results.

The framework gave us a common language to talk about engagement at all levels of the organisation and led to powerful conversations that helped instil a genuine leadership culture. We also found we could use the framework to diagnose problems that emerged and deal with the nuances of different leadership challenges.

Over time, the leaders I worked with added their own insights and approaches. I learned from their successes and continued to evolve the framework — which ultimately became an important foundation for Westpac's leadership development training.

At its most basic, the Leadership Star framework is simple. To build and sustain high engagement, a leader needs to do five things, consistently:

1. *Care:* show you care about people as individual human beings, and that you care about outcomes

2. *Provide Context:* give people meaning by helping them to understand the purpose of the organisation and why what they do matters

3. *Give Clarity:* tell people what's expected of them in terms of their role, outcomes and behaviours — what good looks like, and what great looks like

4. *Clear the Way:* help knock down the barriers that hold people back

5. *Celebrate:* recognise individual contributions and success, creating a powerful feedback loop for performance and engagement.

I've seen these principles work in both my business and not-for-profit activities. And based on the feedback I've received from leaders across business, academia, government and the not-for-profit sector, I believe this framework can help any leader who is committed to building and sustaining a highly engaged workforce.

Beyond the five main points of the Leadership Star, this book also highlights the importance of understanding your own personal motivations, purpose and values, and provides suggestions on how to communicate effectively around each of the five points.

And given the unprecedented economic and human challenges that so many organisations are facing right now, I've also included a chapter with suggestions on building and sustaining engagement in times of crisis.

About me

Since I'm not a trained psychologist or HR professional, it's not unreasonable to wonder how I'm qualified to write a book on engagement.

My first management experience hardly suggested that I had a future in leading people.

While still at university, a family friend offered me a summer job managing an Italian gelateria that she had purchased out of bankruptcy. My job was to get the business going again, including hiring new staff and keeping the former owner (who was employed to make the gelati) away from the cash.

I hired new staff, who ranged in age from 16 to 80, and we got the business going again. But my ability to motivate and lead people was (apparently) woeful: I distinctly remember one young woman screaming, 'You're a terrible manager!' in my face before throwing her apron on the floor and storming out.

At the end of the summer I hurried back to university, convinced that significant people leadership was not on the cards for me.

After graduating with a degree in European History, I joined First Manhattan Consulting Group (FMCG), a boutique management consulting firm that gave strategic advice to banks and other financial services companies.

Five years into my time as a management consultant I was sent to Australia on a project for ANZ, one of the country's largest banks. During that period ANZ offered me the opportunity to directly lead a team of 30 bank employees, on secondment from FMCG.

Although I still bore the scars from my gelateria days, I decided to give it a go — and it changed my life. With a bit more experience and a much greater respect for the craft of people leadership, I 'found my calling', as the saying goes. I discovered that I enjoyed people leadership and, with focus, curiosity and dedication, I got better at it.

Over the next two decades I progressed through a series of senior management roles at ANZ, the Royal Bank of Scotland Group and Westpac, finishing with five years as Westpac's CEO. This exposed me to all sorts of leadership challenges, from how to lead a rapidly growing business (ANZ's credit card business), to how to motivate people in a failed business (RBS), to leading people through a period of extreme external pressure (Westpac).

In addition, the large scope of these later roles, overseeing more than 40 000 people, meant I had to think much more broadly about how to motivate and influence large groups of people when I couldn't personally see — let alone get to know — most of them personally.

At one stage during this period I joined a large international not-for-profit organisation as its Australian chairman, hoping to give back to the community. This experience too ended up teaching me important lessons in empathy and how to connect with people who are driven by a sense of purpose rather than career or financial aspirations.

Through all of these challenges and several crises — including the final regulatory actions, which led to my departure from Westpac in late 2019 — I continued to pay close attention to staff engagement and its drivers. This is because I believe that to sustain good performance and build long-term success, it is crucial that leaders do everything possible to engage the hearts and minds of their people. When you get engagement right, people will deliver more effort and better results in good times, ride out the tough times and encourage other great people to join.

While each situation was different, the large businesses I ran generally saw engagement scores rise to the high 70 or low 80 per cent range, with individual business units — whose leaders followed these principles — frequently scoring in the high 80s or even north of 90 per cent on some occasions. This was at a time where competitor scores (when they published them) were generally in the high 60s or low 70s.

Before we begin, a few caveats ...

While I'm proud of the results that my teams and I have achieved over the years, I'm not claiming to be a perfect leader who has always done everything I'm recommending in this book. Nor am I suggesting that doing these things alone will make you a successful leader.

The Leadership Star sets out an aspiration — one that I've tried to live by but, as I'm sure many of my teammates over the years would agree, I haven't always met. That said, I've found the Leadership Star framework to be helpful when I'm trying to figure out why things aren't working the way they should, and what I personally can do about it.

In calling this book 'a practical guide', I'm acknowledging that leading people in real life can be a messy and imperfect business that doesn't always fit neatly into a framework.

Different situations require different approaches to leadership, and each leader inevitably brings their own personality to bear in different ways — there's no single 'right way' to lead.

Equally, this book doesn't try to cover every aspect of an organisation's engagement plan — how to structure and conduct the surveys, how to calibrate the results and how to tackle each of the issues that may emerge. If this is what you're after, there are a number of independent consultants and firms such as Gallup and Aon Hewitt who are experienced in working with leadership teams and human resource departments on these aspects and can build a tailored program for your organisation.

I also want to be clear that this book is *not* a comprehensive framework for leadership in commercial, government or not-for-profit organisations. Engagement is one useful lever, but other aspects of leadership are at least equally important to an organisation's success, including competitive strategy, financial and balance sheet management, operations effectiveness, technology management, risk management, project management and general human resource management. Each of these is a huge topic in its own right and well beyond the scope of this book.

Finally, while the stories in this book are true, I've changed some of the names and details to focus on the lessons rather than the specific people or circumstances involved. Hopefully by sharing these stories—both good and bad—you'll find ideas and inspiration that help you commit to building high engagement in your team—whether you're an aspiring leader or an experienced CEO.

PART I
The Leadership Star

Care

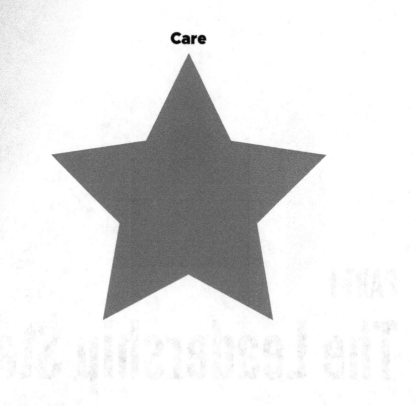

CARE

'Okay, Miriam, I give up. What are you feeding them!?'

Miriam's laugh echoed out through the speakerphone on my conference room table.

I had asked the question in jest, but there was a serious purpose behind it: how was it possible that Miriam's business had 100 per cent staff satisfaction?

The annual staff survey results for the large Australian bank where I worked had just been published, and Miriam's Hong Kong credit card division had returned a perfect score: every staff member had reported themselves as highly satisfied.

There was only one problem with this result: the Hong Kong credit card business hadn't been successful, and Miriam had been sent there specifically to shut it down.

Staff satisfaction of 100 per cent just didn't make sense.

'You HAVE told them we're shutting the business, right?' I'd asked Miriam earlier in the conversation.

'Yes,' she replied.

'And you HAVE told them that they're all going to lose their jobs?'

'Yes,' she said again.

Now I was really confused: our decision to shut the business would have a real impact on the careers and financial security of all of our team members in Hong Kong. It was going to be tough for them, and I assumed morale was bound to take a dive — hence my 'what are you feeding them!?' question.

After Miriam stopped laughing (she has a great laugh, even in tough times), I persisted: 'No, really. What are you doing to get a result like that?'

I'll never forget Miriam's calm reply.

'I speak to every staff member, every day.'

That was not what I was expecting to hear. 'Go on,' I said.

'Well,' she said. 'We're in shutdown mode, so I have a bit of time on my hands. There are 35 people left in the office, and every morning I walk up to someone in the team and say "How are you?", "How is your job hunt going?", "Have you been to see the employment counsellor? What did they say?", "Do you know what you need to do to finish things up?", "Do you need any support to get through it?", "How's your family doing? Are they okay?", "Is there anything more we can do to help?"

'And I have a conversation with them. And then, when we're done, I go to the next person, and say: "How are you?"

'I have that conversation 35 times a day. And the next day I start all over.'

A bit of context: the 35 employees in our Hong Kong credit card business were almost exclusively Hong Kong–born Chinese people. Miriam was an Australian who had been sent by 'head office' to tell all of the staff that their jobs were going, in the midst of a major downturn in the Hong Kong economy.

And yet her people had reported 100 per cent staff satisfaction.

Miriam's explanation over the phone that day gave me the first big insight that ultimately led to me to write this book.

Miriam *cared*.

And more to the point, she *showed* she cared by taking a genuine interest in her employees as individual human beings.

The poet Maya Angelou once said, 'People will forget what you said. People will forget what you did. But people will never forget how you made them feel.'

That's why Care is the first and most fundamental point of the Leadership Star. My definition of engagement is where people make an *emotional* commitment to going above and beyond on behalf of their employer. And it stands to reason that no-one is going to make an emotional commitment to a manager or an organisation that doesn't care about them — that views and treats them as a disposable 'human resource'.

When executed well, Care is not a 'soft' skill. Demonstrating genuine care requires empathy, compassion, self-awareness, authenticity, courage and self-discipline. It doesn't mean you avoid hard decisions and having difficult conversations. But it does mean that *the way you take your actions* reflects genuine consideration for the impact that those actions have on other people.

Greek philosopher Aristotle said successful leadership had three elements:

1. *'Logos' or logic:* how you present the truth, logic and reasons for the actions you are choosing to take.

2. *'Ethos':* your personal credibility, character, reputation and knowledge.

3. *'Pathos' or emotion:* your ability to connect with your people on an emotional level, by appealing to their personal values, fears or aspirations.

In other words, leadership is about being logical, credible and human.

In later chapters we'll talk about the role of logic and character in building engagement. But the true foundation of engagement is human connection.

To build a highly engaged team, you need to *demonstrate* that you care, in three ways. That you care about:

1. them as individual human beings

2. their development and growth

3. results.

Let's look at each of these in turn.

1. Care for individual human beings

When I present the Leadership Star framework to a group of leaders, I like to conduct an experiment.

'How many of you care about your employees?' I ask.

Inevitably, all the hands go up — and I'm sure yours would too.

'That's great,' I say. 'You care about your employees. Excellent. Okay, now let's ask a different question. Let's imagine that you aren't here, and instead I have all of your employees in the room. Now my question is, "Do you believe your manager cares about you?" How many hands do you think would go up?'

The response to this question is always fascinating. Typically, a nervous laugh ripples out over the audience. Then around a third of the hands go up, followed by another third once people have had a chance to look around the room and get embarrassed.

The honest response of these leaders highlights the critical insight about Care.

Care is an *action* verb. It's not a state of being.

I'm sure you care about your people. The fact that you're reading this book says that you want them to be happy and you want your organisation to be successful. But how often do you take *actions* that:

- acknowledge their humanity
- demonstrate empathy and compassion for their situation
- help meet their individual needs?

When I think back over the great stories people have told me about their managers, they have one thing in common: people don't talk about whether their boss met his or her KPIs or brought projects in under budget. They talk about the times their bosses made them feel valued — when they were acting like humans, not just managers.

Let's look at the steps great leaders take to show they care.

Acknowledge their humanity

The first step in demonstrating Care is *acknowledgement.*

My father grew up in a working-class suburb of Chicago and was the first member of his family to attend university. His father worked as a colour engraver on the printing presses at the *Chicago Tribune* newspaper, before adding colour was automated. Every morning he put on a suit, rode the train into the city and then changed into his overalls. He would change back into his suit for his ride home.

After my father graduated from university, he was so keen to work in television that he took a job as a janitor in a TV studio, just to be close to the action, and eventually rose to be the CEO of a television production company. Thanks to his upbringing, he instilled in me the importance of showing respect for everyone you came across in life, no matter their station.

Highly engaging leaders show they care by acknowledging the basic humanity and value of each person they deal with. As a leader, when you smile and make eye contact in the hall, say hello and greet someone by name, you send a simple but powerful message to that employee: 'You matter.'

Conversely, when you're too busy to look up from your phone in the lift, or stare at your laptop in a meeting while someone else is speaking, you send an equally powerful and demotivating message: 'You're not important to me.'

Good leaders don't put up with disrespectful behaviour by the people who work for them either. Bill Swanson, the former CEO of Raytheon, one of the world's biggest aerospace and defence manufacturers, once said, 'A person who is nice to you but rude to the waiter, or to others, is not a nice person.' Some CEOs I know make a point of taking job candidates out to eat, in part so they can watch how the candidate treats others.

When done well, acknowledging people is more than a quick handshake and hello.

Former US President Bill Clinton is famous for the 'reality distortion field' created by his charisma, which is said to make people feel like they are the only person in the room.

In a speech at Harvard in 2007, Clinton related the story of a particular group in Central Africa where the standard response to 'Good morning, how are you?' is not, 'I'm fine, how are you?', but 'I see you'.

It is said that when Clinton meets someone, he silently says, 'I see you' to himself. Whether this is true or not, I can vouch for the way he acknowledges people when he meets them. A few years ago, I had the chance to meet Clinton as part of a small group invited backstage at a conference. I had read so much about his 'reality distortion field' that I was keen to see it in action.

After approaching my small group, he took my hand and held it for a long time, looking me straight in the eye with a smile as I introduced myself.

He then turned and stood next to me, literally leaning against me as he spoke to the next person in the group, occasionally looking back to me to involve me in his conversation with the next person.

The whole effect was extraordinary — here was one of the most famous men on earth, greeting me like I mattered and involving me in his conversation as if I was an old friend.

He certainly taught me the importance of slowing down and making an effort to make people feel special and valued.

You don't need to have Bill Clinton's charisma to build a highly engaged team. But you do need to acknowledge your team members in ways that show you value them as an *individual human being*. For example, do you know:

- their name? Do you know their partner's name?
- whether they have children? Pets? What are their names?
- where they grew up?
- what else is going on in their lives?
- what their hobbies are?
- what they do on weekends?
- where they went on their last holiday, and where they're going on their next holiday?

Take the time to take an interest. It's not hard. Find out who they are, as a whole person. Pay attention: notice how they decorated their workspace. Notice (but think carefully before remarking on) their family photos, the awards and mementos they display, their new jacket, their fitness watch or their new handbag. Depending on the relationship you have with each person you may or may not be able to use these personal details as conversation starters, but noticing alone will help you to know your people better.

When you visit a work location, don't just talk to the manager who is showing you around. Acknowledge everyone you pass in the halls. Talk to the security guard and the cleaners. Stop at random people's desks, introduce yourself, and show your genuine interest in them and what they're doing.

As one of my colleagues once said to me, 'Tell them how much you care before you tell them how much you know.'

Demonstrate empathy and compassion

When you lead a group of people over time, it is inevitable that many of the challenges that come with human life will at some stage find their way into the workplace.

Divorce and relationship breakdowns, parenting issues, caring for an ageing parent, financial challenges, substance abuse, criminal activity, serious physical or mental illness, death of a friend or family member — all of these issues and more will from time to time affect the lives and commitment of employees, either directly or through their relationships with others.

It's not the job of leaders in a commercial organisation to serve as counsellors or therapists for their people, nor should employees see the workplace as a place to unburden themselves of every aspect of their personal lives. Still, the leader who takes the time to demonstrate genuine empathy and compassion for people who are going through tough times can often earn immense loyalty from both the ones who are directly affected and from the broader organisation.

It's remarkable how a few small acts of kindness and compassion can resonate quickly through a culture.

Several years ago, one of our senior operations managers, Sarah, was diagnosed with an aggressive throat cancer. Over several months in the hospital she endured multiple invasive surgeries along with chemo and radiotherapy. Her daughter, Laura, also worked in the business and had just given birth to a baby girl.

After the diagnosis, Sarah's boss, John, reached out to Laura to see how she was coping. A few months later, I received the following email from Laura:

Any old leader will end these check-ins with 'Let me know if I can help …'

But John's care and commitment to serving those around him is so ingrained as part of his values that if there were days here and there that I didn't provide him with an update, he would check in, not expecting one, but just to let me know that he was there.

When Laura's maternity leave came to an end, 'there were weeks during that period that showering was a luxury and a meal outside of a brown paper bag didn't exist', she wrote.

Around this time Laura received a text message from John that said, 'Take as much time as you need, we'll be waiting for you when you're back.'

Laura told me:

It sounds like such a simple thing, but at the end of the day we all know it is the simple and the littlest things that make the biggest difference. My uncle, who made the trip to Australia from Britain to help support us at the time, still raves about what an amazing boss Mum has. He isn't wrong.

Aside from supporting his people when they are ill, John — who has faced plenty of his own challenges in life — sends supportive text messages to team members when their children are taking school or university exams. He knows literally thousands of people by name. He remembers birthdays and career milestones. More than once I've been pulled aside by a staff member who was transferred into his department to be told: 'John is the best manager I've ever had.'

I've known John personally for 25 years and have seen enough to know that this isn't some super-salesman stunt. He genuinely cares, and he makes it a priority to show it.

Is it any surprise that the division John led — Group Operations — had the highest engagement score of any major part of the Westpac Group? I don't think so.

Ironically, sometimes the best way to demonstrate empathy is *not* to do something — particularly when something goes wrong.

Natalie, an experienced event planner in my team, once told me a great story about how a boss earned her loyalty by *not* intervening.

Natalie's boss was in the middle of a large presentation to customers, which involved over 120 videos, the screen suddenly went black. 'I had tested and re-tested every bit of equipment, and yet it suddenly didn't work. It was my worst nightmare,' she said.

'I asked the executive to stay backstage with me while we worked on the issue, but instead he said I knew more about the IT than he did and he trusted me to manage the issue. He then went back to his table. I felt terrible about the technical breakdown and I dreaded what he was going to say to me later.

'We eventually got it fixed, and the presentation went off without a hitch. After the event, I went up to apologise. But he said not to worry. When the guests at his table commented that he must be feeling pretty upset he had told them that if you think *we* feel bad, spare a thought for the team who are trying to fix this.

'It could have been one of the worst nights of my life, but I went home feeling supported and even more committed to doing a good job for him in the future. It shows how a bad situation can turn positive thanks to calm and caring leadership.'

Sometimes the best way to care for someone is to show them that you know they are capable and you trust them, and then stand back and let them at it.

Help meet their individual needs

One important way to demonstrate that you value people as individuals is to recognise and respond to their particular situation and needs.

In the example mentioned previously, John recognised that Laura's allocated maternity leave was not going to be sufficient to deal with the added burden of her mother's illness. Despite not being her direct manager, he also saw that going through the formal process of applying for additional leave (which he would approve, given how valued both she and her mother both were to his business) was an unnecessary burden for her given all the things she had on her plate, so he took care of it for her.

When you've taken the time to really know someone and understand their situation, you will quickly see ways in which you can help them that might be a little 'outside the box'.

In one of my previous roles we had employed a number of disadvantaged young Indigenous Australians in our branches, hoping to give them an opportunity to escape poverty and create a more satisfying career path. One young woman, who was a great worker and good with customers, had started not showing up for work occasionally, without giving any reason.

Her manager took her aside and explained that this wasn't acceptable, and that she either needed to show up or let her manager know when and why she couldn't make it to work so the manager could plan around her. Although she said she understood, she continued to miss work occasionally and the frustrated manager reluctantly concluded that she would need to let the young woman go.

Before making a final decision, however, the manager decided to take her out for coffee and see if he could get to the bottom of it.

It turned out that the young woman's mother was from a remote part of Australia and didn't speak any English. She needed her daughter as a translator on the days that she came to town to do her shopping, and the young woman was too embarrassed to admit this to her boss, so she skipped work instead.

The manager agreed to re-jig the young woman's schedule for those days when her mother needed to come to town, and a high-potential career was saved.

Major projects, urgent deadlines and crises also offer opportunities for managers to respond to individual needs. For example, bank IT projects often require people to work through the night on weekends, when customer activity will be least affected by any interruptions. The best leaders make sure they are personally visible during the night, and think ahead to bring in catering that responds to people's different diets or religious observance such as Ramadan, provide blow-up beds for naps, book taxis to make sure people get home safely and even pay for extra childcare needed to support single parents.

Outside of the workplace, family or parenting obligations, health challenges, military service, religious holidays, cultural or community commitments, exercise or sporting ambitions and volunteering are all examples of individual needs that leaders can support and celebrate as a way of encouraging their people to 'bring their whole self to work'. Flexible working hours, ergonomic or technology changes and special leave are just three examples of ways in which leaders can accommodate these needs.

Rebekah Campbell is an entrepreneur who writes an occasional column for the *Australian Financial Review*. In a column titled 'Why leaders should put people ahead of outcomes (if they really want to succeed)', she tells the story of how a contractor and freelancer had both suddenly let her down on their commitments when she was under a tight deadline — one called in sick, while the other told her that he would be away for a week because his wife was about to give birth.

Intensely frustrated, Rebekah drafted polite but firm emails about the importance of both pieces of work.

Just before she hit send, though, she decided to try a different approach.

She called the designer and told her to focus on getting better. And she sent a baby gift to the home of the freelancer in Bangladesh.

Rebekah wrote: 'I expected pleasant replies, but their responses amazed me.'

The designer was back online later that day with ideas about improving marketing and shifted her other work so she could meet the deadline. The freelancer was astonished Rebekah had sent a gift and became, in Rebekah's words, 'the most committed and professional UpWorker ever'.

A little while later, Rebekah was asked what business advice she wished she could give to her younger self. Her response: 'To care deeply about people and value long-term relationships.'

Obviously, a balance needs to be struck between the needs of the individual and the commercial realities facing the organisation. But when a leader — or an organisation as a whole — encourages people to commit to the organisation *and* makes it possible for them to deal with their challenges or pursue their passions, they reinforce the message that the employee is valued for who they are, not just what they do.

2. Care about their development and growth

The second important aspect of Care is to demonstrate an interest in your people's career development and personal growth.

Organisations are not static, and nor are people. In a highly engaged working environment, people want to feel that:

- they are being challenged
- they are growing in their skills and experience
- their career has a bright future.

It's a symbiotic relationship — increasing the skills and capability of individuals in the team means that the organisation itself can thrive and grow.

The alternative is to view people as merely cogs in a wheel, and not invest in their development. But this is ultimately short-sighted: aside from lower engagement, higher turnover and lower growth will almost certainly offset any savings in time or money that come from this leadership mindset.

Embedding a highly-engaged development culture requires leaders to:

- understand people's abilities and aspirations
- give honest feedback and advice
- invest in their growth.

Understand people's abilities and aspirations

The starting point for helping people grow is curiosity. As leaders we can easily fall into the trap of assuming that we know our people, their capabilities and their aspirations well. But unless you're a mind reader (hint: you aren't), then you won't know until you ask.

Have a conversation with each of your team members, and see if you really know the answer to these questions:

- What's their job history? Where else have they worked, and what roles have they done? What are their career highlights and lowlights?
- What do they like about their job? What do they dislike?
- What do they wish they could change about their role?
- What do they see as their relative strengths and weaknesses?
- How else could they contribute to the organisation, and support you?
- Where would they like to be in five years' time? In ten years? Why?
- How can you best support them in terms of their development?
- What else should you know about them?

While many of these questions may come up in a job interview, it's amazing how quickly we forget to ask people these questions when we work with them every day.

Most people are only in a particular job for a few years. And given the typical rate of staff turnover, that means that, unless they've just started, their leader probably doesn't know that much about what else they've done or where they would like to go.

Moreover, human nature is such that we tend to see people strongly through the lens of today: I distinctly remember my surprise when a consultant I was working with casually mentioned that she had a PhD in consumer risk management — at the exact time I was trying to find a new head of risk. It never would have occurred to me that she had that experience, and if she hadn't mentioned it I would have missed out on one of the best hires I ever made.

Assessing people's strengths, weaknesses and personality preferences is a profession in itself, with numerous tools and executive recruiters in the market that all claim to have the best approach. I've used a number of different tools over time, from detailed behavioural interviews to Gallup's CliftonStrengths and Human Synergistics' Life Styles Inventory™, to

Myers–Briggs personality tests and various Hogan Assessments tools. All of them are useful in getting a better understanding of people's inherent strengths, weaknesses, working style/preferences and development needs — many of which are not obvious from casual conversation or observation.

High-engaging leaders view this as an ongoing process, rather than a one-off exercise. My advice is to schedule regular times for development-focused conversations during the year and, if your organisation can afford it, to re-run a formal assessment process every few years to provide an updated benchmark on how people are progressing.

In doing this, it is critical to agree to and document the aspirations, goals and commitments that emerge from these conversations, so that you can refer back to them over time to see if both you and they are keeping to your commitments.

Give honest feedback and advice

One of the toughest challenges for many leaders is to give constructive feedback to their people, especially when people are not performing well.

But this is an absolute necessity if you want to demonstrate Care.

Many leaders overestimate the negative consequences of giving tough feedback, fearing that it will damage relationships. They assume people don't want to hear tough messages, won't listen and won't change. They also underestimate the benefits of feedback, in terms of helping people improve and actually *strengthening* relationships by demonstrating trust.

Quite simply, you aren't caring about someone when you hold back negative feedback — chances are you're only caring about yourself and the possibility that they will be upset with you.

'Tough love' is an essential part of leadership. If you've taken the time to build your relationship with someone and have shown them that you genuinely value them as a human being, then you've created the groundwork for telling them what they may not like to, but *need* to hear.

I learned this the hard way early in my career.

As a new and inexperienced leader, I had hired a much more experienced executive to lead one of my key departments. While he was very knowledgeable, he also had a way of treating his team and peers that alienated many of them.

When I raised the fact that a number of people had concerns about his behaviour, he pushed back and said that it was, in essence, their fault and that he was simply telling them some hard truths. For a while, I accepted this and made excuses for him when my peers questioned me about it.

Eventually, his relationships with others deteriorated to the extent that I had to exit him anyway. It was messy, and he accused me of firing him to protect myself.

Looking back on the experience, I realised that, deep down, I was afraid to confront him because I genuinely valued him as a member of my team and liked him personally, and therefore didn't want to jeopardise our relationship. But my failure to honestly and forcefully confront his behaviour robbed him of the chance to change his ways and ended up significantly damaging the relationship I was trying to protect.

It also meant that the individuals who worked for him suffered longer than they should have, resulting in lower morale and the loss of some good people who chose to leave rather than put up with his behaviour.

Ever since that experience, I have resolved to be courageous and to give people the feedback they need to hear, even if it risks my personal relationship with them. And what's good for the goose is good for the gander: we all have our blind spots, and I am personally grateful for the many times people who care about me have pulled me up — sometimes brutally — for falling short.

When giving negative feedback, I'm careful not to say things that will destroy their self-esteem. This is easier if you've built trust with the person over time by frequently recognising all the good things people do — a topic we return to in chapter 5.

The challenge is to frame and deliver the feedback so that the person really 'hears' it — as opposed to shutting off. I remind myself to 'tell them how much I care' first, so they know I'm coming from a good place. Occasionally, I will have another person deliver the message if I think they're more likely to accept it from that person than from me. But if they need to be hit hard with a direct message in order for it to really sink in, I'm no longer afraid to deliver a home truth.

You may find it helpful to frame the conversation using the 'AID' model: Action, Impact, Differently. In this approach you start by objectively observing what happened, then talking about the impact of that action, followed by a discussion about how they could handle it differently. For example:

- Action: 'Yesterday in the team meeting you said this about Ted's work.'
- Impact: 'The impact of that statement was that both Ted and his team feel that you aren't supporting their part of the project.'
- Differently: 'While I understand the point you were making, here's how you might have handled it differently ...'

Sharing your own experience and advice with your team members is another way to demonstrate Care, especially if you see someone grappling with an issue that you yourself have faced.

Often the most effective way to give advice is through well-placed questions:

- 'What did you learn?'
- 'How could we have done this better?'
- 'Have you thought about this?'
- 'What are we missing?'
- 'How do you plan to deal with this aspect?'
- 'How can I help you to be more effective?'
- 'What would happen if ...?'

When people come up with answers to questions like this, it makes the advice you're giving them *their* idea.

Try to position your advice so that the listener feels it's in their power to choose to embrace the insight, rather than being told what to do. 'Something I've seen work elsewhere ...' is more effective than 'At company X we did it this way ...'

Remember that sharing stories where things *didn't* go well for you, and what you learned, can also be helpful: showing your own vulnerability builds trust and encourages others to open up when they need help.

Above all, try not to come across as patronising. For many high performers—especially those with big egos—it's far more effective to say, 'may I offer a suggestion' than to say, 'let me give you some advice'.

Invest in their growth

Highly engaging organisations embed skill and career development as a fundamental part of their culture—people are *expected* to work on developing their skills and experiences.

Their mantra, as former US President Dwight D. Eisenhower once put it, is 'Unless we progress, we regress'.

Leaders in these organisations are committed to helping people grow in ways that help both the organisation *and* the individual to succeed. Helping people continue to develop their skills gives a sense of mastery that is a very powerful motivator for many people—who *doesn't* want to feel that they are really good at their job, and are continuing to grow?

Good leaders do this by helping individuals to:

- develop the skills they need to successfully deliver in their job
- build and navigate the relationships needed to succeed in that organisation
- commit to and deliver on the organisation's mission and values.

To create this culture, leaders need to:

- role model a development focus
- invest in training and development resources
- take risks on people.

Role model a development focus

If you expect your people to work on their development, they need to see that it's important to you. This means regularly setting aside time to focus on each individual's development, discussing and agreeing to development goals and the steps required, and following up to make sure that it happens.

Before each development meeting, take a few minutes to consider what observations and advice you can give to each individual to help them grow—they'll notice the care for them that this effort implies, and are much more likely to take the process seriously.

Senior people in particular often feel that they are 'too busy' or 'beyond' needing development or coaching. But if they don't make development a priority for themselves, you can be sure that they won't be effective in making it a priority throughout the rest of the organisation. Whereas many people would jump at the chance to go on a training program or get coaching, with senior people I sometimes have to be quite directive and insist that they take it seriously.

You as a leader need to make your own commitment to developing your skills and capabilities. I'm fortunate that my own innate curiosity (and awareness of my personal limitations) has meant that I'm always reading and trying to learn from others. I've also benefited from working closely with the same coach for nearly 20 years—Barbara knows me well and I trust her completely to give me honest feedback. From time to time I've used other coaches as well who bring particular skills and insights that have helped me deal with difficult situations and grow as a leader.

Throughout my career I've been open with my team about the role that these coaches and mentors have played in my life. This is because some people see coaching or training as a sign of weakness, and I want to send a message that working on yourself is not just okay, but essential to leadership success.

Another good way to demonstrate your commitment is to include group development activities in your leadership agenda for the year. This could include:

- setting aside development days led by outside facilitators to work on team dynamics

- inviting outside speakers to address team meetings or participate in Q&As

- asking each person to do a 360-degree review and share the results with the team

- conducting site visits as a team to your own or others' facilities

- sending team members on a study tour, with a report back to the team.

These shared experiences can be very effective at generating new ideas, increasing knowledge and skills and strengthening relationships among team members.

Invest in training and development resources

Investing in specialised training resources is a good way to demonstrate your commitment to people's development. This can include giving people access to third-party online training sites, putting dedicated trainers in each area, building your own internal training academy, and sending people to programs run by business schools such as Stanford, Harvard, INSEAD and the Australian Graduate School of Management.

The scale of your investment will necessarily depend on your organisation's resources and ambitions, and more expensive training resources can be limited to high performers or people with high potential. However, training doesn't have to be overly expensive: low-cost online resources have proliferated in recent years, and some of the most effective training comes in seminars developed by senior leaders or experienced high performers within the organisation itself.

While informal training and coaching sessions are an important part of the mix, from an engagement perspective it's surprisingly important to formalise the development program and resources in some way. If you don't do this — and regularly remind people of the resources that are available — then they can easily forget that it's there and lose sight of the expectation that they continue to work on building their own skills and experience.

Take risks on people

Two decades ago, a former consulting client of mine offered me my first large management job, running ANZ's 1000-person credit card business. He was taking a huge risk: until that point, I'd only temporarily managed a department of around 50 people, and most of my real management experience was in leading small teams of consultants.

Luckily for me (and him!) the risk he took worked out well — we grew the business several fold over the next few years, and I went on to have a successful career leading a series of larger banking businesses.

I will always be grateful to Peter for the risk he took in recommending me for that job — it changed my life. And ever since I have tried to 'pay it forward' by taking risks on people in whom I see something special.

It hasn't always worked: if you truly care about an individual, sometimes you need to say no to risks that they want to take. For example, they may not have the skills to succeed in the role, or the leadership experience to cope with a highly complex or political situation. In these situations, putting them into the role could be setting them up to fail.

But most of the time you do people a great service by pushing them out of their comfort zone into roles where they will grow as professionals and as people. The secret to deciding when to push people is to identify their underlying strengths and weaknesses, and think about how those could apply beyond a role or function that they've already performed.

Executive recruiters and hiring managers often make the mistake of looking for someone who has done a particular role or demonstrated a particular skill before they will give them the opportunity. I look deeper to identify the person's underlying skills, character traits and development needs, and then look for lateral moves or step-up opportunities that both suit those skills and address those needs.

For example, I once appointed an operations executive named Susan to run an offshore joint venture we had set up with an overseas bank. Susan was not an obvious candidate for the role: her experience was mostly in operations, and she hadn't worked on the sales or marketing side of the business. She wasn't well known among senior management in the bank. And Susan herself would admit that, at the time, she was rather a rough diamond, with a thick regional accent and a less-than-highly-polished dress sense.

The joint venture partner was dubious when I introduced her. But the more I thought about it, the more convinced I became that she was the right choice: Susan knew the operational details of the business cold, and this was going to be important in this market. She had a track record of spotting great young people in her team and developing them rapidly. She was incredibly hardworking, a single mother and personally courageous. She had come from limited means and worked her way up to a senior role in the bank. Her family background gave her an insight into the culture she would be going into. And above all, she was passionate and forceful in expressing her desire to be given a chance.

Susan nailed it. Within a few short years the business had grown dramatically, and the shareholding was eventually sold back to the partner for more than ten times the initial investment. The joint venture partner loved her and didn't want her to leave when her tour of duty was up. And Susan grew into a polished and successful senior banking executive, with a number of senior roles around the region.

If people believe that you see their potential, and if you are willing to push them and take risks to help them develop, you will build great loyalty and their personal engagement will soar: they will believe in you and the organisation, since you and the organisation believed in them.

For the organisation overall, the benefits of Care as a leader extend beyond staff loyalty, engagement and retention. Leaders who take the time to demonstrate Care for their people set a standard that inspires their team members to care about each other as well — a habit that rapidly extends through the organisation (and in some cases, improves people's family relationships as well).

3. Care about results

Caring for your people as human beings, and caring about their development, are both important inputs to creating a high-engagement organisation.

But to sustain high engagement, you need to care about the outputs as well.

You need to care about results.

Unlike school, there's no 'partial credit' at work. You either get something done well and on time, or you don't. You either meet your targets, or you don't. The consequences of a failure to deliver for your customers, your competitive position or your shareholders are usually clear.

As a leader, people need to see that you are committed to excellence and delivering results. This is because success breeds success: a team that consistently achieves stretching goals is more likely to feel proud and confident in its capabilities, and as a consequence to become highly engaged. This helps attract other high performers to join the team, and encourages the team to take on even greater goals.

Leaders need to be simultaneously cheerleader and coach — revving up the team and encouraging a player whose confidence is shaken, while not being afraid to give tough love to a player whose head isn't in the game or bench the player who isn't delivering on the day.

There's a line to be walked — bullying or intimidating people over results is never okay, and bullies are poison in a healthy and highly engaged culture. But leaders should never apologise for striving for excellence and making the tough decisions needed to achieve it.

The best people want to be part of the best team — some of my best hires came when I met a high performer at a competitor and explained that my goal was to build the best team in the industry, and I saw them as part of it.

So don't be afraid to declare your aspiration, and go find the best people you can.

And remember that leaders who demand and expect excellence from themselves set a standard that makes all of their people better.

In *The Last Dance* — the 2020 Netflix documentary on the Chicago Bulls' 1998 championship season — Michael Jordan gives a fascinating insight into his mentality as team captain and how he treated his teammates:

> *When people see this, they're going to say 'Well, he wasn't really a nice guy, he may have been a tyrant.' Well, that's because you never won anything. I wanted to win, but I wanted them to win and be a part of that as well.*

You don't have to have Michael Jordan's ferocious competitive spirit to be an effective and engaging leader. But people do need to see that you care — about them, and about what they achieve.

When you show that you care about results, you send a message that the work your organisation does is important, and that what your people do matters.

Without saying it explicitly, you're also giving your people *Context*.

And that's the focus of our next chapter.

CARE

Summary

Care is the foundation of a highly engaged culture, in three respects. You as a leader must Care:

1. for your people as individual human beings

2. for their development and growth

3. about results.

While most leaders would say they care, it's important to remember that care is an *action* verb—you have to demonstrate care through what you say and what you do.

Questions for reflection

- How well do I really know each of my team members as people?

- Would they say that I care about them?

- What actions have I taken recently to show it?

- Am I giving people sufficient constructive feedback, or am I pulling my punches?

- What further actions could I take to increase their awareness?

- Is personal and career development a key part of our organisation's culture?

- How else can I embed development thinking into my leadership rhythm?

- Am I demonstrating sufficient Care and commitment to our goals?

- How else could I challenge people to lift their performance and standards of excellence?

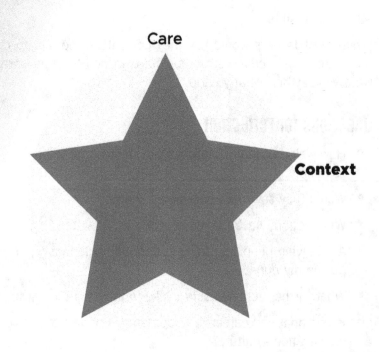

Care

Context

2

CONTEXT

A man was walking down the road when he came across a building site. Soon he came to a worker on his knees, laying bricks.

He asked the man, 'What are you doing?'

'I'm a bricklayer,' said the man. 'I'm laying bricks.'

A bit further along he came to another worker, standing alongside a partially built wall.

'What are you doing?' asked the man.

'I'm a bricklayer,' said the man. 'I'm building a wall so I can feed my family.'

He then saw a third man, up on a scaffold, rapidly adding bricks to a wall. This man moved much more quickly than the other two workers and seemed from his body language to be genuinely enjoying his work.

'Hello there!' he called up to the worker. 'What are you doing?'

'I'm building a cathedral,' called back the worker. 'I'm serving God.'

The story of the three bricklayers neatly summarises the power and benefit of giving people a sense of purpose in what they do. One worker has a skill and gets paid to use it. He's indifferent about what he's building and just happy to have a job. Another recognises that his skill supports his family's wellbeing. He's working hard so he can keep the job and continue supporting his family. But he'd probably leave if someone offered him more money to go elsewhere.

The third bricklayer, however, feels connected to a higher purpose — building a cathedral in order to serve God. His satisfaction comes from knowing that his work is contributing to something important and lasting — that is important to him personally — and he is the most productive of the three. It seems unlikely that he'd leave this job to chase a few more dollars somewhere else.

Highly engaging leaders know that building a sense of purpose among employees is critical.

If you're asking people to put in and sustain an extra effort — to do more than show up and perform a task in return for pay — then people need some other form of motivation. They need to see that what they do is part of something bigger. They need *Context*.

Each person brings their own intrinsic motivations to work. Their financial situation or personal history may mean they're simply grateful to have a job that keeps a roof over their head. Or, like the second bricklayer, they may be motivated by their ability to provide for others. War memoirs are full of stories of soldiers performing selfless, heroic acts out of a commitment to their 'brothers' in their platoon. High-profile management consulting firms and investment banks are able to draw on a seemingly endless supply of driven young graduates who are happy to work long hours in return for the prestige and status that comes from working for a McKinsey or Goldman Sachs.

But companies like these are the exceptions. And even a McKinsey or Goldman Sachs needs to find other things to motivate their staff once the 'prestige' halo wears off — as it inevitably does.

Likewise, relying on a competitive hiring process to build a team of highly self-motivated individuals is unlikely to result in sustained high performance. Personal priorities can change over time, so leaders who rely on self-motivated teams will likely spend a disproportionate amount of their time stroking egos and responding to spot fires of low morale.

To build a highly motivated and consistently engaged team, leaders need to help their people find *meaning* in their work — a sense that they are contributing to something important, that is bigger than themselves.

This starts with the leader themselves: leaders who demonstrate an authentic passion for the purpose of the organisation create an energy that is contagious, while those without that sense of purpose have the opposite effect.

For employees, this sense of meaning comes when they:

- *understand* the company's purpose
- believe that the purpose is *worthwhile*
- believe that the purpose is *aligned* with their own personal values and goals
- see how their *personal efforts help* achieve that purpose.

Leaders, particularly at more senior levels, often take the understanding of purpose and meaning for granted since they have better visibility of the organisation's 'big picture'. But their team members don't automatically have that same view. That's why it's important to provide — and continually reinforce — context on:

- the organisation's purpose
- the organisation's priorities
- how each individual's role helps achieve the purpose and priorities.

In the following sections I'll share a few thoughts on each of these aspects of Context, along with a few observations on what works and what doesn't in articulating Context to your team.

What's your *why?*

Many organisations have an official purpose or mission statement[1] as part of a 'Mission, Vision and Values' framework used in strategy presentations. And while each of these elements forms part of an

---

[1] For some good examples, HubSpot's blog (blog.hubspot.com) has an article titled '17 truly inspiring company vision and mission statement examples'; for some bad ones, Inc.com has 'The 9 worst mission statements of all time'.

organisation's context, the starting point for high engagement is the ability to answer the question, 'Why are we here?'

In his widely viewed TED Talk, Simon Sinek makes a compelling case for the 'Golden Circle' of 'Why, How and What' — with 'Why' at the very centre — as the starting point for inspiring action. And *action* is the key word here: many vision statements are so high-level and divorced from the daily life of employees that, while they may briefly inspire people, they rapidly lose relevance and impact on engagement. That's not to discount the role of vision statements in general: they also play an important role in strategy development (although that is beyond the scope of this book).

Chances are that your organisation already has a public mission, purpose and/or vision statement. These words are often used interchangeably, depending on the organisation, and the structure of the statements is often similar. For clarity, in this book I prefer to focus on 'purpose'. To me, purpose is about *why* your organisation exists, whereas mission statements tend to describe *what* you do and for *whom*, rather than *why*.

For example, at its founding Microsoft's mission statement was 'to put a computer on every desk and in every home'. Today, Microsoft's official statement speaks more to purpose: 'To empower every person and organisation on the planet to achieve more.'

From an engagement standpoint, it's the *why* that really drives emotional connection.

When building engagement, it's worth considering whether the existing purpose statement has the right characteristics to drive engagement. Having been involved in defining purpose statements for a number of businesses and teams over the years, I've learned a few things about what works and what doesn't.

Be realistic

First, the purpose needs to reflect the reality of the company and its situation. 'To organize the world's information and make it universally accessible and useful' makes a lot of sense when you have the technical capability and credibility of Google. And if you have the innovative, out-of-the-box culture of a Zappos.com, you might be able to get away with 'To live and deliver WOW'.

But if you're a bank in the middle of a price war, then 'We help people achieve their dreams' might sound good to the marketing department but is unlikely to have much credibility with the broader organisation when they are in the middle of another wave of cost cuts. Much better to focus on something credible — one of my personal favourite statements was from Pest Control of Naples: 'We kill bugs.'

Orientation: inside or out?

Second, there's a choice to be made on the extent to which the purpose is internally or externally oriented. In other words, does the stated purpose focus on outcomes for the company or outcomes for its customers and the broader community?

Internally oriented purpose statements often focus on the quality of products and services or a company's relative position in the marketplace: 'to build the most reliable electric bikes'; 'to be the nation's best online guitar retailer'; and 'to be the leading supplier of semiconductor fabrication solutions' are examples of this approach.

In some cases, an organisation will include an explicit focus on its people, their wellbeing and/or their commitment to sustainable business practices as part of their purpose; for example, '... to provide a dynamic and challenging environment for our employees'.

The other common internal purpose focus is on profitability or shareholder value creation. Some investors subscribe to Milton Friedman's argument that 'there is one and only one social responsibility of business — to use its resources and engage in activities designed to increase its profits'. As an example:

> *The purpose of the Cooper Tire & Rubber Company is to earn money for its shareholders and increase the value of their investment. We will do that through growing the company, controlling assets and properly structuring the balance sheet, thereby increasing EPS, cash flow, and return on invested capital.*[2]

---

[2] Found on missionstatements.com, 'Fortune 500 mission statements', however this no longer appears on the Cooper Tire website. Coincidence?

While a purpose statement like this might be effective in engaging stock market investors, it's unlikely to be helpful in engaging a workforce.

I agree that growing shareholder value should be a primary objective of for-profit companies. However, in my experience even the most mercenary investment banker doesn't get out of bed each day because they're excited about creating shareholder value.

In any event, the assessment of 'value' depends heavily on the time frame of the investor. If — as in the case of a bank — the majority of a company's value is in its long-term earnings capacity, then value creation will depend on its ability to continue to perform for its customers over time.

There's nothing wrong with a purpose statement that focuses solely on the company and its achievements. But this limits the extent to which people can be truly inspired to contribute. Unless an organisation is in trouble — and therefore focused purely on survival — the more externally oriented the purpose can be, the better.

Externally-oriented purpose statements focus on the *outcome* of what the organisation makes or does: providing improved performance or quality of life for its customers, or in some way making the world better for its stakeholders. The clearer and more vivid this statement is in describing the desired outcome, the more compelling and motivating it tends to be:

- 'To accelerate the world's transition to sustainable energy' (Tesla)

- 'To reinvent how people share knowledge, tell stories, and inspire their audiences to act' (Prezi)

- 'To brighten the lives of seriously ill children and their families' (Starlight Children's Foundation).

Buzz off

The final observation is to avoid buzzwords and corporate-speak wherever possible. The more buzzword-laden the phrasing, the more it becomes noise to employees. Ideally, the statement should be clear and simple enough that every employee can recite it by heart — not because it's mindlessly drummed into them, but because they get it, and it resonates with them.

As an example, which of the following statements do you think is more likely to motivate and be remembered by staff?

- 'To bring safe water and sanitation to the world' (Water.org)

- 'To entertain, inform and inspire people around the globe through the power of unparalleled storytelling, reflecting the iconic brands, creative minds and innovative technologies that make ours the world's premier entertainment company'.

That the latter statement is from the Walt Disney Company shows that a simple statement is not necessarily required to run a great company. But it seems unlikely that many people outside of the C-suite would find this statement a daily motivation.

What 'purpose-driven' looks like

The best example of a purpose-driven company that I've experienced is USAA. It's a member-owned insurance and financial services organisation that primarily serves US military and government employees and their families.

USAA is well known in the financial services industry for the quality of their service and high customer satisfaction — Net Promoter Scores are typically four times higher than the industry average.[3] Famously private, USAA rarely allows outsiders to visit, but several years ago I was invited to spend a day meeting with members of senior management at their San Antonio, Texas, campus.

When I arrived in the morning, I was ushered through security by a woman who introduced herself as my host's assistant.

'USAA is a military organisation,' my guide explained as we walked. 'We serve the people who serve.

'And that's really important to me,' she went on, 'because I'm from a military family. My dad was in the military, and my brother is in the military. In fact, one in four of our call centre operators have a military

---

[3] See forbes.com, '5 customer experience lessons from USAA'. 'Net Promoter Score' (NPS) is a common measure (and registered trademark) of customer satisfaction/engagement popularised by Fred Reichheld and Bain & Company.

connection — either they've formerly served themselves, or they're from a military family.'

Impressed with this background, I arrived upstairs at the conference room where the first senior executive was waiting to greet me.

'I'm Johnny,' he said, shaking my hand. 'I run IT here. At USAA, we're a military-focused organisation. We serve the people who serve.

'And that's important to me and my team,' he continued, 'because many of our members are serving overseas, and IT is the only way they can reach us. If one of our members is on a mountain in Afghanistan, and his wife's car breaks down in Arizona, he does not want to have trouble reaching us. So our target is 100 per cent uptime. Not 99 per cent. Not 99.9 per cent. One hundred per cent. And we're almost there.'

For the rest of the day, every single executive came into the meeting and told me a similar story, starting with 'we serve the people who serve' and going on to link their and their team's role, in their own words, to the corporate purpose.

Now *that's* Context!

Finding your organisation's purpose

But what if your organisation doesn't have a purpose statement, or you're concerned that the current statement won't be effective?

If you're the chairman, CEO, or leader of an independent business unit, developing or refining the company purpose statement should be within your control. This situation is a gift, as it allows you to involve staff at all levels in the company in talking about the future and what is important to them in terms of how they see the company's contribution.

A purpose statement that genuinely reflects the values, aspirations and motivations of the employee base is far more likely to stick.

Ultimately, though, the purpose statement needs to be something that you personally believe in and find motivating; if it ends up as more corporate spin, people will see right through it.

In my experience the best result comes from conversations with your team, where you whiteboard ideas and scrutinise the pros and cons of each.

This can be done through a series of meetings with senior executives, or a broader initiative where all employees are encouraged to engage in the discussion based on a company-wide survey of current and desired values.

Remember though that 'a camel is a horse designed by committee' — beware of the tendency of groups to fall back to corporate-speak or trying to please everyone. As CEO, you can and should ultimately make the call, as you are the ultimate owner of the corporate purpose. Keep chipping away until you have a tight statement that you can repeat endlessly to staff and still feel inspired to action each time you repeat it.

If you're not senior enough to design your organisation's purpose statement, try creating a subordinate purpose statement that is more genuinely motivating for you and your team. On the one hand, it's important that all of your team see how they link to the overall corporate purpose (CEOs tend to get cranky if they see people re-inventing things that are rightly within the purview of senior management, such as mission or purpose statements). However, where a business is operating under a different brand from its corporate parent, or the corporate purpose is a statement of high principle, most CEOs will accept that an individual unit needs to interpret the corporate purpose into something more actionable and engaging for its people.

The Westpac vision statement

When I became CEO in 2015, Westpac's vision statement was 'To be one of the world's great companies, helping our customers, communities, and people to prosper and grow'. But given the importance of purpose to both strategy and engagement, we decided to review this statement to make sure it continued to resonate with our strategic direction, our customers and our employees.

This statement had been in place in one form or another for nearly 200 years. Founded as the Bank of New South Wales in 1817, Westpac is Australia's first bank and oldest company. From reading the founding documents of the company (Westpac maintains an impressive historical archive), it was clear that the original founding purpose of the bank was to support the development of a private economy in the then penal colony of New South Wales.

I felt that this historical legacy lent authenticity to an externally-oriented purpose statement focused on helping—and helping was something that we knew resonated strongly with Westpac staff, who had a track record of exceptional generosity of spirit in volunteering their time to support the community, whether in times of crisis such as droughts and bushfires, or for Indigenous community advancement, or fundraising for chronic disease.

Westpac's corporate activities were also aligned with this spirit of helping, through a 45-year partnership with the iconic Westpac rescue helicopter service, its corporate support for organisations such as Jawun, Dress for Success® and the Bread & Butter Project and its various sustainability policies. It also had a 20-year track record of global recognition for its leadership positions on climate and social policies. Helping a community to 'prosper and grow' is clearly aligned with the economic role of a bank, and by including 'our people' we acknowledged that the sustainability of a large institution is clearly tied to its ongoing ability to attract and develop great talent in a competitive employment market.

The one change we did make was to add the word 'service' to the purpose statement, which then read as: 'To be one of the world's great *service* companies, helping our customers, communities, and people to prosper and grow'. There were two reasons for the change: first, the focus on service was the central idea of our corporate strategy, and adding the word brought more alignment to our various internal communications. Second, without the word 'service' the statement could be read as overly internally oriented—and maybe a bit self-aggrandising ('one of the world's great companies'). By contrast, a 'service company' is one that by definition exists for an externally-oriented purpose—and is only 'great' if its customers believe it's great.

This purpose statement worked well to engage our people. In my experience, most front-line retail and commercial bankers get their deepest satisfaction from the relationships they build with their customers. The focus on service rather than 'sales' better aligned with the personal values of most banking staff. The statement was also general enough to cover all of the bank's different lines of business, while still feeling directly relevant for each business. It wasn't overly generic, as the idea of focusing on service signalled a clear break from businesses seeing themselves as product or sales businesses. It tied in with the bank's history, which I constantly reinforced to give the statement legitimacy and help build pride among the staff. It recognised the symbiotic nature of a bank with its customers, communities and staff. And it was aspirational—everyone knew we had a long way to go to achieve world-class service.

Although the statement is arguably a bit long (and no doubt my successors will continue to look for ways to simplify it), I found that it struck an effective balance between internal and external orientation. Over time, most staff could repeat it back to me almost word for word, and the importance of delivering great service became embedded in every business and function.

One challenge Westpac had was its multiple brands—St.George, Bank of Melbourne, BankSA, RAMS and BT Financial Group all had their own histories and cultural variations. However, we found that the core purpose was clear and relatable enough that each brand was able to position their own purpose within this broader context: BT Financial Group selected 'Helping Australians prepare for their best financial future', while Bank of Melbourne's stated goal is 'to help you and your business "make it", because as you prosper, so will our local communities, and the state. Your success is our success'.

Define your priorities

The second aspect of Context is to help people understand the organisation's priorities. This is important for several reasons:

- *It helps an organisation to be more effective.* People's efforts are aligned to the most important priorities, rather than dispersed across many issues.

- *It helps individuals make better choices.* Each individual makes their own prioritisation decisions about how to spend their time and, in the case of managers, their resources. The clearer they are on the organisation's priorities, the better choices they will make.

- *It helps people understand senior management decisions.* Senior management often involves making hard choices among several good ideas — choosing 'right from right'. By understanding the organisation's priorities, people are more able to cope when something good or important isn't being funded or prioritised.

Note the focus on priorities rather than strategy. Executives often feel compelled to share lengthy discussions on strategy with their people. This instinct isn't surprising, given it takes up such a large focus for senior management and the board.

However, the word 'strategy' means many things to different groups: some think in highly academic terms about gaining competitive advantage, while others treat the word 'strategy' as a synonym for 'goals' or 'priorities'.

For a broader audience, detailed strategy discussions can actually reduce an organisation's focus and confuse people. My suggestion is to keep strategy discussions relatively high level — a couple of sentences on what trends are facing the industry, where the company is looking to compete and how it intends to win is usually sufficient.

The more relevant issue for most people in an organisation is the organisation's strategic priorities. Ideally, these are three to five simple statements (any more and no-one will remember them) that describe specifically what the organisation is trying to achieve, and by when.

For example:

- to become #1 in customer satisfaction within three years
- to lift our Return on Equity to 12 per cent by the end of next year
- to complete an injury-free year
- to sign up 1 million new online customers by December 31
- to open 50 new store locations by the end of the third quarter
- to complete migration to the new accounting system by July 31.

Structured correctly, 'what by when' provides people at all levels with the basis to link their actions and decisions to the organisation's overall objectives — it guides them in their daily life and helps them feel connected to the greater corporate purpose.

This notion of connection is the final piece of the context puzzle.

Individual roles

'I'm just a teller.'

Over years of visiting branches, I lost track of how many times I heard this response after asking a staff member what they did in the branch.

To me, it was a clear sign that their bank manager wasn't doing their job properly. To my way of thinking, the teller was arguably the most important person in the branch, if not the bank: they had the most frequent interaction with customers and were the face of the bank for many customers.

Although banking is increasingly an online experience, customers' impression of the bank's commitment to service is often set by how friendly, accurate, efficient and helpful the teller was the last time they visited a branch. The best tellers greet all of their customers by name, can recognise when a customer is being scammed, and have been known to follow up on the health of an elderly customer who hasn't been in for a while. They're the first line of defence against fraud and carry an enormous burden in making sure that a bank meets all of its compliance requirements.

Disney resorts are famous for the amount of training they give their staff—especially the street cleaners. Disney recognises that street sweepers are arguably more important to the guest experience than Mickey Mouse himself: few people ask Mickey where to find the Pirates of the Caribbean, but hundreds of people every day will ask a street sweeper. The street sweepers are also the eyes on the ground for management—they can see what is working, and what isn't. And they can deliver 'magic'—for example, showing a family with young children where to stand to better view the passing parade.

It's the job of the leader to make sure that everyone in the organisation understands why their specific job—what they do all day—is important to the organisation's success. Too many leaders forget that this isn't obvious to new (or even long-time) staff members who don't have the same level of experience and exposure to senior management. If people clearly understand that link, it gives meaning to their daily activities.

That doesn't mean that they will necessarily enjoy every aspect of their job, but it does give them the self-respect that comes from knowing that the company, and its customers, are depending on them. That they are part of something bigger: building a cathedral, rather than laying bricks.

Putting it into practice

To embed Context in the organisation, it's important to think both about:

- when to address the topic
- how to bring it to life for different groups of employees.

When to talk about Context

Context discussions typically happen at several levels. Large organisations often hold town halls or other big meetings on a regular basis, where senior leaders provide a strategy update, talk about recent performance and lay out the priorities and targets for the period ahead. These sessions are an obvious place to provide a context overview—at least in terms of purpose and priorities.

Induction sessions for new staff are another important opportunity to share Context on the organisation's purpose: at Westpac, every new staff member is required to attend a session on their first day where, among other activities, they watch a video of the CEO talking about the company's values, history, purpose, strategy and culture.

Senior leaders should also make a point of regularly coming back to Context — including the priorities — in formal and informal discussions with staff, and in written communications. Over time, I found that as CEO this became second nature and was a great place to start in laying the groundwork for whatever specific topic I wanted to address with various groups.

In written communications, this means starting with a reminder of the organisation's purpose and then explicitly linking the topic at hand to that purpose. At Westpac that included printing the organisation's purpose statement at the start of each monthly board report, and at the start of annual shareholder communications.

In group meetings, it's helpful to refer to the purpose as part of the answer to a question or in explaining the rationale for whatever is being announced or discussed. This reinforces that your commitment is 'real' rather than just rote repetition of a corporate slogan.

Tailor the Context

For both front-line and senior people, the linkage between specific roles and the purpose of the company is generally easy to understand. Senior leaders have good access to the organisation's strategy and priorities, and know where they and their team fit in. Similarly, front-line staff get direct feedback from customers on how they are using the organisation's products or services and can see how their personal efforts are contributing.

Strategy and mergers and acquisitions teams generally have no problem seeing the link between their work and the corporate purpose. Similarly, marketing, corporate affairs and digital teams usually have good exposure to customer research and have a level of involvement in shaping the organisation's products or service experience — although this link can get weaker as you get deeper into these functions.

It gets more complicated in behind-the-scenes roles, such as operations and technology, and corporate functions, such as finance and legal.

Operations and technology areas sometimes fall into the trap of focusing so closely on financial and operational metrics that they lose sight of the end customer. Unless they are speaking directly to the customer by phone or digital message, the actual product or service of the organisation can seem quite remote. This can be further compounded when an operational area is physically remote from the main business, for example, through an offshore or outsourced vendor arrangement.

Ironically, the value of Context becomes even greater in these circumstances. In my experience, people who work in repetitive environments *want* to find meaning in what they do all day, and leaders who directly provide that context find that they are rewarded with tremendously engaged and energised teams. At Westpac, for example, the highest engagement score among large areas of the company was consistently in the operations team — a fact that often surprises outsiders and reflects the incredible focus and care from its senior leadership.

In areas such as finance, legal, human resources, audit and risk, the link of an individual's daily work to the purpose of the company may seem tenuous. Language is worthy of attention here: legal teams can choose to refer to 'customer issues' rather than 'matters', while HR teams can measure and discuss 'employee wellness' rather than simply the 'lost time injury frequency rate'.

Make Context real

A number of other interventions can help overcome this challenge. First, leaders in these areas can bring to life the end-customer impact of what their people do. This could take the form of visits, videos, or brown-bag lunches with customers to see how customers are using the organisation's products or services and to brainstorm with the team how they can better contribute to the corporate purpose. Many companies require all employees to regularly join customer visits or even be trained to take calls during peak periods.

As an example, Westpac's IT department regularly runs what they call 'ImagineIT, DoIT' days. In these sessions, large numbers of the

IT staff visit branches and various other teams across the company to understand, log and fix their IT issues — no matter how small. A central team of experts takes calls and identifies fixes for typically hundreds of issues, many of which are completed that same day.

Exercises such as this serve the dual purpose of helping technology staff appreciate how their work affects the lives of front-line staff and their customers, as well as giving front-line people an appreciation for the amount of support and investment that stands behind them.

Train for Context

Another approach that works well is focused training to reinforce the message that 'we are all part of a single, connected service experience'.

This approach focuses on highlighting the hand-offs and connections between different parts of the company. Through large sessions and smaller team activities, staff are asked to identify specific other people or teams in the organisation on whom they rely for their work, and who rely on them. They then meet with people in those areas to better understand what they do and how their own work affects the work of those other areas. This tends to 'lift the horizon' for people and help them build stronger connections to the organisation and its customers.

Another version of this is a company 'fair' between departments. This takes the form of a half-day session where each department puts together a 'booth' with a short presentation on what they do, with employees moving around every 20–30 minutes to learn about other areas and make connections. When based around a fun theme like Halloween, and finished off with staff drinks or a barbeque, these sessions can go a long way to building connections and shared purpose.

Is it working?

Leaders often wonder — with justification — whether their presentations and communications are making an impact on their people's daily lives.

Staff surveys and comments can obviously help answer the question of whether key messages are resonating. 'Word clouds'[4] based on feedback in surveys on questions related to purpose can help identify alignment or misunderstandings, while frequent 'pulse' surveys can include questions on whether the staff member understands the organisation's purpose and feels personally aligned to and motivated by it.

Another important indicator of progress is in the language used by the staff themselves. Listening closely to the answers of open-ended questions such as 'tell me about your business' and 'what are your people focused on' will give you a good sense of whether the sense of purpose is flowing through the organisation. If their answers include mention of the corporate purpose or use similar words in describing their own team's work, you know you're on the right path.

Asking people what they're proud of is another way to see if their priorities match up with the company's overall agenda. With enough focus and consistency, you'll see key words from the purpose statement begin to show up in the stories they tell of their achievements internally and on social media such as LinkedIn.

These formal and informal soundings on purpose should be taken at all levels in the company and across different business and functional groups. And don't forget to include key business outsourcing partners — especially if they include teams of people who speak directly to customers or staff.

If front-line people don't feel that their managers and internal service providers are acting consistently with the corporate messaging, they quickly become sceptical and disengaged, assuming it's another round of corporate sloganeering that will soon pass. This is why asking senior and mid-level managers to explain the company purpose to you and how they relate to it personally is just as important as discussing it with the front line.

---

[4] A word cloud is a visual representation of key words in text responses, with the size of the words reflecting their frequency in the text.

CONTEXT

Summary

Chapter 1 highlights the importance of caring for each person in your organisation as an individual human being. Part of that Care is acknowledging that most people have choices about where they work, and that to be committed to an organisation they need emotional rewards that go beyond pay and benefits—they need to feel that what they do is meaningful.

To create meaning, leaders need to give people Context that helps them link their personal goals and values to the organisation's purpose. In doing this, they empower employees to make their own choices and personal commitment to their work, rather than relying solely on the leader for ongoing motivation.

This means leaders need to help people understand:

- Why the organisation exists—what is its higher purpose? In what ways does it serve its customers, and the broader community?

- What are the organisation's priorities?

- How does each individual's daily work help deliver those priorities?

- Why is it worth doing—how does it align with each individual's own goals and values?

Leaders can't assume that this context is automatically understood, and it needs to be continually reinforced. But when a company gets it right, the strong emotional connection between organisations and their employees leads to tremendous pride, commitment and energy that is hard to beat.

Together, Care and Context create the atmosphere that's necessary (but not sufficient) for a highly engaged organisation. In the next three chapters we look at how organisations can translate that latent goodwill into sustained high performance and engagement.

Questions for reflection

- Does our organisation have a clear purpose statement?

- Is it simple to understand? Does it resonate with me personally?

- Does it resonate with our people? Is it motivating?

- Does the purpose statement reflect an external focus, or is it all about us?

- Why should employees feel good—personally—about working here?

- Does everyone in the organisation understand our top priorities?

- Does everyone—both front-line and functional roles—understand how their role links to that purpose?

- Does everyone understand why their department and role is important?

- How and when do we reinforce this context to our people—both new and experienced?

- How do we know if the context messages are getting through?

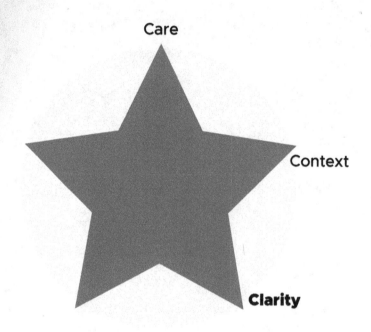

CLARITY

'This is a dumb process — I hate it!'

Damien, my HR director, just looked at me and tilted his head, a nervous smile showing he had some sympathy for me, but not much.

It was performance review time — the end of my first full year as a divisional business executive — and we were now engaged in the annual corporate ranking process.

It was the classic big-company approach — each executive was given a numerical performance rating of 1 to 5, along with a 'behaviour' rating of A, B or C. 1A was the best, while 5C meant you weren't going to be around to receive your rating.

In addition to a rating, each person was ranked relative to everyone else at their level, and this ranking drove their annual compensation result. The underlying goal was to drive a performance culture by paying the top-ranked people (typically the top 20 per cent) the biggest bonus, mid-level people less and the bottom-ranked people no bonus at all.

My task was to 'force fit' the executive team into a proportional distribution.

'But this is a ridiculous review process,' I responded. 'We've had a great year, and all of my executives have beaten their goals. How am I supposed to rank them?'

'I get it, but you have to,' Damien replied. 'The bonus system is designed to reward the top performers. And the problem isn't the review process. The problem is your target-setting process at the start of last year.'

The penny dropped, and I realised he was right.

It was true that each of my executives had beaten their targets — but it was also true that those targets weren't adequate to discriminate among them: who had a good year, and who had a great year. Whose targets were set relatively low, and whose were truly stretching. Who benefited from good market conditions, and who overcame tough obstacles to achieve their results. Who role-modelled the corporate values, and who was a pain in the neck to deal with.

I was worried about the ranking process being seen as unfair because people could only judge their own performance based on what was in their performance document. On that basis, each of them would think that anything other than a top ranking outcome was unfair.

In this case, my failure to clarify expectations better upfront made the performance assessment process more difficult.

High performance — and high engagement — requires Clarity in three respects:

1. *Role Clarity.* People need to understand exactly what their job is — what's the scope of their responsibilities, what are they accountable to deliver and what authority do they have to make decisions?

2. *Goal Clarity.* What specific outputs or objectives are they meant to accomplish, and over what time frame?

3. *Behavioural Clarity.* How are they expected to behave in the workplace, while delivering on their goals? Given the desired culture, what behaviour is okay and what isn't?

While this may sound obvious, it is remarkable how often managers fail to give this level of clarity to their direct reports and their broader organisations.

Lack of clarity is often at the root of underperformance and poor execution: missed profit targets, inefficiency, excessive bureaucracy, failed projects, ineffective teamwork or poor personal behaviour.

Meanwhile, a team with great clarity often achieves much more than it even thought possible.

Let's look at each aspect of Clarity.

1. Role Clarity

Chapter 2 highlights the importance of helping each individual understand how what they do all day contributes to the broader mission. That linkage is an important aspect of role clarity. But to build true engagement and effectiveness, it's important to go deeper.

Some liken a good business to a finely tuned machine, where each of the parts performs its specific function well and meshes with each of the other parts in turn to produce high-quality products and services that people will pay for.

The analogy is imperfect, since most businesses are in fact *organic* — the 'parts' are human beings — with all the uncertainty that entails. Plus, in business the 'machine' needs to respond and adapt constantly to a changing market and competitive environment.

Without real clarity on who is doing what, the business machine can't operate efficiently. In most businesses, Clarity comes in a job description document that provides each employee an overview of the role along with details on their:

- formal job title
- reporting line(s)
- responsibilities and duties
- required skills and qualifications for the role.

There are typically hundreds (if not thousands) of distinct job descriptions in large organisations, usually prepared during the recruitment process and largely forgotten once an appointment has been made. These documents also tend to fall into one of several traps:

- they are so high-level and full of corporate-speak that they provide little useful guidance to the employee, and are thus largely ignored

- they are so detailed that they overwhelm the employee's ability to carry the information in their head as a practical reference, and are likewise largely ignored

- responsibilities overlap or are unclear, so that people in related functions either both think they are accountable or assume someone else is.

The move to agile and other forms of team-based working has seen many leaders reject the perceived bureaucracy of job description statements in favour of more informal working arrangements and self-guiding teams based on a small number of generic roles such as 'product owners', 'scrum masters' and 'development team members'. And while these approaches do offer great improvements to delivery efficiency and engagement for many teams, it's a myth to think that they don't still require great role clarity and structure in order to achieve their goals.

I've seen many leaders make the mistake of assuming that role clarity is obvious.

Having grown up in the organisation, they may have personally performed many of the roles in their structure. Or, they assume that — having recruited someone with the same job title from another organisation — the new person must know what's expected of them. This can be compounded by individual employees' desire to look competent, a cultural pressure to fit in, or a reluctance to admit what they don't know — especially if they want to impress a new boss.

This is a dangerous mistake that sets both the individual and the organisation up for failure.

For the individual, lack of role clarity can lead to:

- spending time on the wrong things

- missed deadlines

- not meeting quality requirements

- failing to build effective relationships with important colleagues.

It can also lead to personal stress and burnout, particularly when people sense that they may be failing and work excessive hours to try to meet unclear expectations from their leader.

For the organisation overall, turnover statistics[1] mean that at any one time nearly a third of staff are new to their roles or new to the organisation — so a large percentage of team members may be working ineffectively and below their potential as they try to learn the ropes. Lack of organisation-wide role clarity can also raise the risk that important safety, compliance or quality checks fall between the cracks.

On a positive note, good clarity can lead to more autonomy (and therefore engagement). As the saying goes, 'good fences make good neighbours'. Or, to use a sporting analogy, the fact that the rules of the game are clear doesn't stop a great player like Michael Jordan or LeBron James from innovating on the basketball court.

It's therefore critical that, at the start of every new job or assignment, team leaders meet with each employee to make sure they understand their role in detail, *both as an individual and as a member of the team*. This means clarifying:

- what their specific accountabilities and expected outputs are

- where, when and with whom they are expected to work

- how their role fits into the broader team — including how any matrix reporting arrangements are meant to work

- what authority they have to make decisions, and when and how they should escalate a decision to their manager or others

- what budget and other resources they have to work with

- what their safety, code of conduct and compliance obligations are

- what formal meetings or other governance processes are required

---

[1] According to the Australian Bureau of Statistics, the median Australian job tenure for those under 34 is less than three years.

- what steps they are expected to take when they have a question or an issue

- how and how often they are expected to report on their progress.

Although this might seem a long list, giving role clarity doesn't have to be a complicated or bureaucratic process. Nor am I suggesting that you micromanage experienced people.

While it does require a degree of pre-work by the leader to clarify their own expectations, the ideal process is simply an in-person conversation where the leader outlines their expectations in plain English, and encourages the employee to ask questions so that they fully understand the scope and expectations of their role.

A record of this discussion—with key points noted in plain English—can then be formally acknowledged and kept as a useful reference for the individual employee and the manager. This 'performance contract' between the leader and the employee can also be used as a reference during regular performance discussions.

It can also be helpful to hold team discussions from time to time where people share their expectations and workshop how decisions will be made, and conflicts resolved.

All of this assumes that the person is qualified to do the role or can quickly become qualified through the right training and coaching. Nothing damages engagement or performance faster than having the wrong people in roles—for example, in roles where they can't play to their strengths, have misaligned values or behaviour, or lack the passion for their work that leads to discretionary effort.

It's a truism among former business leaders that the most common regret is not moving fast enough on people who weren't suited or weren't performing in their roles. It's beyond the scope of this book to discuss the assessment and appointment process in detail,[2] but having the right team in place is necessary, if not sufficient, to build a high-performing, highly engaged organisation.

---

[2] See for example *Topgrading (How to Hire, Coach, and Keep A Players)*, by Brad and Geoff Smart.

2. Goal Clarity

At the start of a new role or assignment, leaders typically meet with each employee to discuss specific goals or delivery targets for the period ahead. Most organisations use a balanced scorecard to document these goals. This scorecard is then used as the basis for assessing performance and giving feedback, and potentially for determining career progression and annual compensation.

While the bones of this approach are common across most organisations, the extent to which the process works to drive performance and engagement varies widely. As with job descriptions, I've observed a number of traps with this 'standard' approach:

- *Too many measures.* If the scorecard is more than two pages long, it will be ignored (or filed away and forgotten until a few weeks prior to the next performance review).

- *Targets are too high.* If the performance goals are seen as out of reach, they can demotivate rather than motivate the individual. Depending on the environment, they can also lead people to cut corners or cheat in order to 'meet their numbers'.

- *Targets are too low.* This can undermine overall performance, with mediocre performers falling into complacency, and high performers looking elsewhere for challenge and recognition.

- *Targets are too generic.* In the interest of 'fairness', leaders sometimes set common sales, service or productivity targets for all staff in a given role. If legitimate differences in opportunity exist (for example, in high-growth versus low-growth locations), this can lead to *both* of the previous two traps — since targets are too low for those in high-opportunity areas, and too high for others.

- *Targets conflict.* A lack of coordination on goal setting among leaders can mean that teams or individuals fight for similar resources or fail to support each other where needed to achieve their respective goals.

Goal setting is one of the most frequently occurring and important aspects of leadership. And yet few leaders have been trained in how to do this effectively, or spend much time doing it. Some may see the process as too far 'down in the weeds', and delegate it to finance or the human resources department. Others are exhausted from the last performance review process, and just want to get on with delivering next year's result.

As the story at the start of this chapter illustrates, I've come to believe that a leader's personal time spent on goal setting at the start of a period more than pays for itself in both results and engagement. Having struggled through this myself over two decades, I've learned a few things that make a difference in setting effective targets:

- explain why the goal is important
- distinguish between good and great performance
- realise that not everything is a target
- clarify lead versus lag indicators
- reinforce a growth mindset.

Explain why the goal is important

In chapter 2 we discuss the importance of providing the overall Context for the organisation and why each individual's role is important. Goal setting is a critical opportunity to reinforce this link and bring it to life for people. Try to build an emotional link for people by showing how the goal links to a higher, external purpose: for example, by serving customers, colleagues or the community at large.

Sometimes there's an obvious and direct link between the goals that are set and the organisation's mission: for example, customer satisfaction goals and a corporate mission around service.

But in other cases, those links need to be spelled out more clearly. Why do safety targets matter so much to a mining business? Why are detailed quality checks so important to an auto parts manufacturer? Why are so many documentation checks required on a mortgage application? If this link isn't spelled out clearly, there's a risk that employees won't take them seriously.

Or worse, if the goals you set aren't aligned or even conflict with the organisation's purpose, people will rapidly become cynical about your actual commitment to the organisation's mission.

For example, if the Context narrative is all about providing great service but the goals are all about sales numbers, employees will rapidly draw their own conclusions about what the organisation's purpose really is.

Distinguish between good and great performance

The key to effective goal setting is helping the individual know the answer to two questions:

- What does *good* performance look like for the period ahead?

- What does *great performance* look like?

Good performance is about meeting expectations in the role: by the end of the period, what are the specific things that the individual should have accomplished in order to be seen by their boss to have a done a good job? That could include specific sales, service or productivity targets, completion of certain projects or deliverables, meeting key budget or risk constraints, demonstrating improvements in their own teams, and so on.

In this context, 'good' performance implies two things:

1. That the individual's contribution is commensurate with their share of the task required to meet the broader team or organisation's goals.

2. That it meets the leader's expectations for what an effective, dedicated employee with equivalent skills in a similar context ought to be able to achieve.

In a high-performing organisation, 'good' performance should still require significant effort and effectiveness — it's not meant to be a low bar. It should be pegged around the level that, all things being equal, will mean that the individual achieves their contractual compensation expectations and enjoys continued career growth.

Typically, 'good' performance targets include a number of financial, sales or operational targets that have been cascaded down from the overall group or divisional targets. In my experience, pragmatic managers add a buffer of say 5 to 10 per cent to the overall target before further cascading it to their teams. That buffer means that the overall team result can still be achieved in the event of an unexpected issue arising in the business or a significant performance 'miss' by part of the team.

Great performance is more subjective, but it's equally important to clarify.

The idea is to tap into the psychological magic of 'stretch' thinking.

Help your people to stretch

US President Kennedy's speech to Congress in May of 1961 is a classic example of the power of stretch thinking — leading as it did to the first moonwalk in July of 1969, and the achievement of Kennedy's stretching target:

> I believe that this nation should commit itself to achieving the goal, before this decade is out, of landing a man on the moon and returning him safely to the Earth.

In essence, the idea is to set a goal that is sufficiently stretching that, on the day it is set, no-one in the team — including the leader — is sure that it can actually be accomplished, much less *how* to accomplish it. Great performance *requires* you to come up with a different way of doing things in order to achieve it: a new product or customer angle, a new process, new people in key seats, or the application of new technology.

If the goal is sufficiently clear — and sufficiently different from the current reality — it creates what psychologists call 'cognitive dissonance'. In plain English, the human brain gets upset by the difference between the goal and today's reality — and works to reconcile those differences.

Some of that work happens consciously, as people brainstorm ideas and think logically about possible solutions to achieve the goal. But importantly, the *unconscious* mind is also enlisted in the challenge, often leading to more creative solutions.

The original Sony Walkman, for example, was famously engineered after the CEO put a block of wood in front of his engineers and told them to 'make me a player this big'.[3]

---

[3] See *The Illusion of Leadership: Directing creativity in business and the arts* by Piers Ibbotson.

Properly applied, setting 'stretch' goals (or 'BHAGs' — Big Hairy Audacious Goals) is a powerful technique for both engagement and performance.

When online banking was first introduced in the late 1990s, my colleague Chelvi, who led the online business, set the goal of onboarding 1 million online banking customers by year end. At the time this seemed a crazy ambition: online shopping itself was still in its infancy, and Amazon was still mostly known as an online bookstore.

That 'One Million Online Customers' target — posted in large letters on the wall, staring down at everyone along with a daily update of the actual number — inspired great people to join the team, and drove a sense of urgency and creativity that saw the target achieved ahead of time.

But how do you determine the right amount of stretch?

If the stretch is too low, it won't force fresh thinking and may lead to mediocre or even deteriorating performance over time. At the very least, you'll miss an opportunity for real growth.

On the other hand, if the stretch is outlandish and unachievable, it can cause people to switch off or become demotivated. Worse, it can lead to adverse cultural impacts such as hiding or falsifying information that shows people aren't meeting stretch goals — the story of Elizabeth Holmes, CEO of Theranos, detailed in the book *Bad Blood* by John Carreyrou, is a great example of how *not* to drive a culture of stretch.

While the *right* target is a judgement, there is one question that I have found to be extremely helpful in calibrating the level of stretch: 'What stretching goal, if we achieved it, would make you immensely proud?'

This formulation triggers the subconscious mind to generate an initial answer that often hits the mark. It connects both the head and the heart.

In my experience the 'right' answer to this question has three characteristics:

1. *It's scary.* If the target doesn't cause an involuntarily clenching in your stomach, it's probably not tough enough.

2. *It has a nice ring to it.* Large, round numbers — 10 per cent, 50 per cent, 200 per cent — and statements such as 'doubling' or

'halving' something—are much more likely to be remembered and get buy-in.[4]

3. *It grows on you.* The more you repeat the goal, the more it creates a warm glow and aspiration about how proud you will feel when you accomplish it.

Note that this question can and should be asked from both a 'top down' and 'bottom up' perspective.

As the leader, it's part of your job to challenge your team to achieve more than they thought possible. The 'performance envelope'—what people can actually achieve—can typically be pushed way beyond what people think. Therefore, working out what *you* think is the right answer is a good place to start. Leaders have a broader perspective about the organisation or team's overall goals and competitive context and are therefore best placed to determine what needs to be accomplished.

That doesn't mean, however, that the leader needs to have the right answer on *how* to do it. In a modern, fast-moving world, that's rarely the case.

Team discussions to set the right stretch target can help identify new ideas and shape your thinking. To bring these ideas to life, you might try distilling these ideas into a mocked-up article in *The Economist*, dated several years hence, that describes what the team has achieved.

Just be careful not to fall into the trap of setting stretch by consensus. That's a recipe for watering it down towards good rather than great performance. Rather, challenge your people to find out what they're capable of. And at the end of the day, *you* as the leader need to decide.

Some of the best individual stretch goals emerge in one-on-one conversations with people where they are asked to decide what the right stretch goals are for them. While some people are understandably reluctant to over-promise, my experience is that individuals generally do step up and articulate goals that meet the criteria described.

---

[4] Note that aspirational phrases such as 'world class' or 'the best', while good in purpose statements, don't lend themselves to goal clarity and should be avoided in this context.

In practice, I like to explain the importance of stretch thinking and then articulate those criteria before asking the question.

You'll know when it's worked: the person will articulate a goal that grabs you, and then make an 'uh oh!' face, since they realise how challenging it's going to be.

And then the wheels start turning, and the innovation begins.

Realise that not everything is a target

As Jim Collins, author of *Good to Great: Why some companies make the leap while others don't*, said, 'If you have more than three priorities, then you don't have any.' One of the classic mistakes in performance measurement systems is to translate every aspect of the job description into a performance target.

Performance management systems can take a number of forms. A typical 'balanced scorecard approach' defines a series of measures and sub-measures that are each given a weighting that cumulatively add to 100 per cent, with a weighted average performance score calculated at the end of the period. For a complex role, this can get seriously out of hand — I've personally seen scorecards that ran to 30 pages of measures.

Other organisations follow an 'OKR' approach (Objectives and Key Results), where high-level objectives (for example, 'Become market leader') are then broken down into a series of key results (for example, '#1 national market share in our category') and initiatives (for example, 'Launch a new advertising campaign').

This approach has the advantage of clearly linking targets and context. For example, a bank branch manager might be able to say:

- our organisation's objective is to lead on service

- as a branch manager I need to increase the service quality delivered by my people

- this quarter my key initiatives are training and returning calls by end of day

- my targets are to go from 60 to 95 per cent of calls returned by end of day.

The downside of this approach comes when the leader's instinct for perfection or completeness leads to a long list of OKRs and initiatives.

Having too many performance measures makes high engagement hard to achieve. This is because:

- if there are too many measures, the person simply can't keep them in their head. Humans simply can't remember a list with any more than seven items in it — and fewer than five is better. If you have to refer to a long document to remember everything you're supposed to be doing, the likelihood of self-confidence and success is low.

- lots of measures means that each specific measure has very little weight — so people tend to spread themselves very thin across each item, thereby limiting their impact.

- not everything is assessable. Many of the aspects of roles are fairly binary: you either do it, or you don't. The opportunity for any sort of stretch performance (or poor performance for that matter) can be quite limited. How, for example, does a leader meaningfully distinguish between the performance of people whose job is to deliver a monthly computer-generated financial report? Rather, it's reasonable to assume that if people have been well screened for their role and understand their job description, any gaps in the basic performance of their role can be dealt with if and when they emerge.

Most people in modern organisations confront a complex and ever-changing set of priorities, some important, some not, and many of them 'urgent': what author and consultant Chris McChesney calls 'the Whirlwind' in the book *The 4 Disciplines of Execution*.

From a management execution standpoint, identifying one or two 'WIGs'[5] is a key discipline to make sure that people focus their discretionary effort where it can make the biggest difference to the delivery of the team's overall goals.

While more than three measures is counterproductive from a day-to-day execution standpoint, from a performance management point of

---

[5] 'Wildly Important Goals' are a key element of the 4 Disciplines framework.

view it's not unrealistic for people to have clear goals across a slightly larger number of categories, with a few specific measures under each.

In appendix A I include a discussion of the approach to performance management and target-setting that I've developed over my career as I've sought to strike the right balance between simplicity and complexity on the one hand, and objective versus judgemental assessments on the other.

The development and exercise of judgement is fundamental to good leadership. I've found that people will generally accept (if not always like!) your judgement as long as:

- they feel that their perspective has been heard by you
- they believe you've considered this perspective fairly and without obvious bias
- you acknowledge their perspective and explain your decision while saying explicitly that it is a judgement.

This approach forces you to get clearer in your own mind about what your expectations actually are — and communicating your judgement helps the individual to get clearer on what they need to do to succeed. Over time, this gives people a greater sense of control of their destiny (thereby further improving engagement).

Clarify lead versus lag indicators

So far this chapter has focused on bringing Clarity to the goals leaders set for individuals as part of an organisation's performance management process.

However, there is another, more immediate notion of goal clarity that helps build both good execution and delivery disciplines *and* engagement.

This is the concept of 'lead' versus 'lag' indicators, as described in the book *The 4 Disciplines of Execution*.

In this framework, 'lead' indicators are measures of *activity* that are within the control of the individual or team: for example, the number of sales calls made, files that are processed, or lines of code that are written. These measures are generally tracked on a near real-time basis and reported at least weekly.

'Lag' indicators are *outcome* measures — such as sales volumes, market share, customer satisfaction scores, or return on investment — that are typically set as goals in a performance management document. These measures are typically reported less frequently — monthly or even annually — to align with financial reporting or performance management time frames.

The idea is to select one or two lead indicators that will have the greatest impact on delivering on the 'stretch' lag indicators, and then set goals for each — with progress tracked and reported in a weekly team meeting.

In this process, each individual makes a weekly commitment as to what they personally are going to do to drive the lead indicator in the week ahead, knowing that they will have to explain their progress in next week's meeting.

I've seen this process work very well to align efforts within a team and move the performance dial. But it also helps to increase engagement, both by giving people a sense of control and by giving them the positive reinforcement of frequent wins (rather than waiting till the end of a long performance period for the lag indicator to come through).[6]

This more focused day-to-day approach to goal clarity can sit neatly within a broader performance management framework: the selection of one or two lead indicators gives focus to an individual's (or team's) discretionary effort, but that doesn't mean that a broader set of expectations and targets can't apply to a given role over a longer performance period.

Reinforce a growth mindset

Goal clarity is about more than cascading a set of objectives from the top down through an organisation. While top-down goals create a level of certainty, they can also be demotivating if the individual doesn't feel capable or empowered to achieve the goals.

---

[6] See chapter 5 for a discussion of the value of frequent wins. To learn more about how to apply the lead and lag methodology, see *The 4 Disciplines of Execution*, by Chris McChesney, Sean Covey and Jim Huling.

Involving people in setting their own goals helps encourage a 'growth mindset' — the belief that one's intelligence and talents can be developed through dedication and hard work, rather than being 'fixed'. Dr Carol Dweck at Stanford University first popularised this concept in her study of what motivates students. Her research has demonstrated that nurturing a growth mindset leads to increased motivation and achievement.[7]

People with a growth mindset come to:

- see challenges as opportunities to be creative
- accept failure as the precursor to learning and improvement
- see criticism as a gift that gives them alternate perspectives
- find value in the process as well as the end result.

An employee with that mindset is almost by definition highly engaged. And an organisation that embeds a growth mindset is far more likely to see creativity, job satisfaction and personal fulfilment as hallmarks of its culture.

For a leader, the keys to building a growth mindset are threefold.

First, there's a level of basic education for leaders and employees about what it means to have a growth mindset, and why it works. This includes training on how the brain works and what specific practices and habits people can employ to shift their own thinking.

Second, goal setting and performance review processes need to be redesigned to reinforce a growth mindset. At Westpac, we radically overhauled the annual review process, replacing it with Motivate — a new process in which each employee sets and commits to their own goals in monthly Motivate discussions with their leader.

Under Motivate, end-of-year incentives are based on the individual's performance against their Motivate goals, rather than on formulaic pay-for-performance calculations.

Finally, the demonstrated behaviour of the leader and their team is critical.

---

[7] Check out her TED Talk, 'The power of believing that you can improve'.

Moving to a growth mindset requires a genuine shift in thinking for many people, and some leaders need to change decades of embedded habits around how they motivate people — moving from judgement and criticism to a more challenging and supportive role that leaves the employee in charge of their performance.

Highly engaging leaders demonstrate that they are committed to helping their people to achieve their goals and to grow as people. They take an active interest in their team's learning and development. They set and articulate high standards, demonstrate confidence that their people can get there (with the leader's help where necessary) and hold people to account when they fall short.

The leader's own behaviour is addressed in more detail in chapter 6, but for now it's a good segue to the final clarity aspect that leaders need to define: what behaviour is expected.

3. Behavioural Clarity

While high engagement is an important marker of a good culture, I have personally found that the word 'culture' means so many things to different people that it isn't all that helpful in itself to building engagement.

'Culture' tends to be expressed as high-level aspirations, for example:

- a customer service culture
- a high-performing culture
- an achievement culture
- an ethical culture
- a collaborative culture
- a strong risk culture
- an open and honest culture
- a fun culture
- an inclusive culture.

Statements such as these don't provide enough granularity about exactly what behaviour is expected of people. And high-level statements can often be used to justify behaviour that works *against* engagement (for example, the bullying manager who uses the 'high-performing culture' tag to justify berating team members who miss their targets).

It's more helpful to think of culture as an *outcome* of behaviour. And if you want a strong (and engaged) culture, you need to provide real clarity on what behaviour is desired, and what isn't acceptable.

I like to think about behavioural expectations in two categories:

1. At a base level, what are the *minimum acceptable standards* for all employees?

2. At a broader level, what are the *underlying values of the company*, and how do these translate into expected behaviour?

Code of conduct

The first category is the organisation's code of conduct, touching on basic expectations. This can be in terms of:

- personal conduct and respect towards others (including externally)
- requirements for meeting legal and regulatory expectations
- expectations around use of company property, including internet and email
- commitment to maintaining confidentiality and customer privacy
- safety and environmental standards.

A clear and concise code of conduct is an important foundation for every organisation. The discipline of having each employee sign an acknowledgement of this code when they start, and re-acknowledge it on, say, an annual basis, provides ongoing clarity to staff and helps quickly resolve any problems that do emerge.

Define your values

Once basic behavioural expectations are clear, the bigger challenge is to articulate the aspiration for how individuals will behave and work together effectively to achieve the organisation's purpose.

This is where the organisation's *values* come into play.

While 'values'—like 'culture'—mean subtly different things to different people, I use the term to mean the fundamental principles that underpin the organisation's purpose. If these values are well chosen, they serve as a reference guide to the organisation on both how to make decisions and how to behave.

However, espousing values that aren't reflected in clear behavioural expectations can lead to cultural cynicism that undermines engagement.

Early in my career I visited the headquarters of a major bank client whose 'Company Values' were etched in a giant glass plaque that hung over the lobby. Over time it became a source of great amusement for me and my colleagues—and many of the individuals who worked there—that every time you went upstairs in that building you observed the exact *opposite* behaviour to what you'd seen described in the lobby.

While I'm sure you have had your own experience of 'values hypocrisy', it would be a mistake to write off a genuine focus on values as wasted effort.

In fact, if the organisation's values are explicitly translated into behavioural expectations that everyone understands, they provide the foundation for a culture that is genuinely aligned to the mission.

The process for doing this is straightforward but does require effort from both the leader and each team member.

If you're the CEO of an organisation that doesn't already have a values statement, there are a number of paths you can take, ranging from a 'top down' approach (where the CEO and/or their top team simply defines the list of values) and a 'bottom up' approach (where a survey of workers' personal values and their 'desired' organisational values helps to define the list). Whichever approach you take, make sure the resulting list is well aligned with the organisation's stated purpose.

If the values are already well defined, the CEO and top team need to consider whether to run with what's already in place, or to modify or replace the existing values.

This is obviously a judgement call, but my advice is to change values only reluctantly.

When you change the values, you're sending a message to existing employees that the fundamental principles of the organisation they've joined no longer apply, or weren't really that fundamental in the first place. That's a good way to make them feel less connected to the organisation in the future, and more likely to be sceptical about the permanence of any 'new' values.[8]

A related pitfall for top teams is where individual business units have — or want to have — their own set of values that are different from the corporate list. This is an understandable desire for leaders who want to build esprit de corps within their team and shape their own culture.

As CEO, my strong belief was that there could only be one set of values for the company. To have more than one set undermined the benefits of consistency and alignment that a values-driven organisation could achieve.

The only exceptions were where an operating unit was essentially being run on a separately branded, arms-length basis — in essence as an investment rather than as part of an integrated or closely connected business. Even in these circumstances, permitting a separate set of values makes it more difficult to move people seamlessly around the organisation and works against broader engagement, as the lack of common language around values (even if the underlying meaning is similar) can reinforce an internal us-versus-them dynamic.

Define the behaviours

Regardless of how the values are arrived at, the next step is a team discussion focused on the values and how they translate into expected behaviour. This step is critical because it helps surface differences in interpretation and perception and builds consensus and commitment among the top team to what 'living the values' means in practice.

---

[8] Unless it's a true turnaround situation, a better approach may be to gradually evolve the values list, with one or two changes per year following significant consultation and communication with staff, to allow them to see the change as *their* idea.

This conversation—which typically takes place over a couple of hours—should take place out of the normal team meeting environment, whether in an offsite location or simply a different room setup than usual. The goal is to build emotional commitment and buy-in, so it's important to put people in a more open and reflective mood, without the time pressures and constant interruptions of mobile devices. A separate facilitator—if well chosen—can help keep the team focused and on track.

The desired output of the meeting is a table—crisp enough to fit on one page—that comprises three columns, as shown in table 3.1.

Table 3.1 Expected behaviour

Organisational value	What it is	What it isn't
For example, 'Integrity'	List (in plain English) of actions/behaviours that are consistent with the value, for example: 'Always meet my commitments' 'Give honest feed-back regardless of the consequences'	List of behaviours or actions that are not okay or consistent with the value, for example: 'Covering up mistakes' 'Shading the truth' 'Seeking personal advantage'
'Customer First'	...	...
'Accountability'	...	...

While the exact words aren't that important, it's worth spending time as a leadership team to develop the right examples. Corporate-speak and platitudes ('people are our most important asset') should be avoided at all costs. By talking it through, teams will come up with their own specific examples and evocative phrases that can be used to reinforce expectations in later situations—thereby making it much more likely that everyone walks out of the room with a shared view of what is acceptable, and what isn't.

For example, in a conversation about how we would demonstrate 'Care' as a value, one of my colleagues related the tradition among cyclists to 'shake the water bottle' — reminding everyone else in the peloton to have a drink. From then on, 'shake the water bottle' became a catchphrase for team members to remind each other to look after themselves physically and emotionally when they could see their colleague was under stress.

Once this table is finalised — typically by the leader, who needs to fully own it — it becomes the reference point for everyone in the organisation. It should be distributed widely, discussed in similar sessions by every team (who are encouraged to develop their own specific examples of what's okay, and what isn't), and embedded in the performance appraisal and feedback process — which is a critical aspect of defining and reinforcing Clarity.

Bear in mind that people can often be particularly cynical when a new values statement gets rolled out. The most successful leaders prevent this by fostering an honest discussion about the extent to which people believe the organisation is currently living these values, rather than simply trumpeting the values through a slick presentation or corporate video.

Putting it into practice: feedback and consequence

So far, the discussion on Clarity has focused on steps taken in advance — when someone is appointed to a role, and at the start of each performance period.

But maintaining Clarity requires ongoing effort: market or internal developments can mean that priorities change in the middle of a performance period, and issues can emerge in business or personal life that distract individuals or teams from their true priorities.

It's also important to calibrate and recalibrate from time to time the degree of stretch asked of each individual.

A well-designed performance feedback and consequence framework is essential to embed the clarity needed to drive high engagement. Unfortunately, many large organisations have allowed their review processes to devolve into bureaucratic box-ticking that actually undermines engagement.

To avoid this risk, effective review processes include a number of aspects that help build engagement and support a growth mindset among employees, including:

- a sense of control for the individual
- frequent check-ins
- a behavioural component
- separating absolute from relative performance
- consequences.

A sense of control

If the individual is given a sense of control over their performance assessment—as already discussed, this includes asking the individual to provide input to their stretch goals, as well as a broader discussion about their priorities and targets—they should feel heard and invested in the outcome.

Frequent check-ins

The second aspect is to include frequent interim discussions where the individual reports on their progress and updates their near-term priorities. This is important because it helps the individual see a close link between their role description, their goals and their day-to-day activities. If conducted frequently, these check-ins also reinforce the importance of rigour and discipline in driving long-term results.

Psychologically, these sessions help the individual take personal accountability for their results (especially if they focus on lead indicators), and frequent feedback helps them course-correct before the end of a performance period. (At Westpac there are monthly Motivate meetings for all staff where managers review performance against Motivate goals that are formally tracked in a system.)

A behavioural component

The third aspect is to formally incorporate assessments of behaviour as well as performance goals. This inevitably requires a level of judgement, but my experience is that practice makes this easier over time and it often leads to breakthrough coaching and motivational sessions.

My approach to assessing behaviour is to assign each individual a rating of A, B or C against each of the agreed values as part of the regular performance cycle. (An example of what this form looks like, and its link to the goal assessment, is in appendix A).

The scale is as follows:

- A: role model for this value
- B: lives the values, no major issues
- C: issues to discuss.

The way I explain this approach is as follows. Everyone on the team has been hired and screened for the values. Therefore, we should expect that people are living the values, and most people should be assessed as a B; in my book, a B is a perfectly good rating on behaviour.

Occasionally, some people stand out consistently through their actions — for example, they might be the sort of person who is endlessly going the extra mile to resolve a customer's issues or are unbelievably caring and proactive when a staff member is off sick. These are the sorts of people who will get an A on a particular value — they are the dictionary definition of that value in our context and recognised as such by their peers.

A persistent or egregious violation of the values will likely lead to dismissal, so performance reviews become moot. However, none of us are perfect and occasionally someone will have ongoing issues with living up to one or more values — and that will need to be addressed.

A rating of 'Issues to discuss' makes people more likely to remain open-minded and listen to feedback than if they thought they were failing and about to be fired. As the leader, you can simply say, 'there's an issue here, and you need to address it' rather than falling into the trap of arguing over evidence. If each individual value has its own rating, then a 'C' on one value doesn't have to mean that they lose their overall 'B' rating for behaviour — but the individual is left in no doubt that they need to improve.

To reinforce a growth mindset, start the formal review discussion with behaviour — at Westpac it's the first piece of paper in a review document. The leader assigns an overall A/B/C rating for behaviour, and then a numerical rating for goal achievement, with a table outlining the goals as page two of the document. If the goals have been set properly, there should be little debate about the goal ratings, because the individual will already know how they did on most metrics.[9]

Separating absolute from relative performance

The fourth aspect of a good review process is to separate *absolute* from *relative* performance in the discussion.

For compensation and career progression, many organisations use a bell curve distribution to rank their performers into various cohorts — the top 10 per cent, followed by the next 20 per cent and so on. If absolute and relative performance are seen as the same thing, this works against a growth mindset, since it sets employees up in opposition to each other — making 'winning' the goal, rather than rewarding achievement or doing your very best.

Another danger of this approach is when the leader or HR team themselves game the system in order to reverse engineer a desired relative ranking. This is extremely demotivating for individuals, who will feel their contributions aren't valued and the leaders aren't trustworthy — a disaster for ongoing engagement.

A better way is to have two separate conversations with the individual. In the first, you focus exclusively on how that individual performed against the goals that were set, both in terms of targets and behaviour. This discussion is about support, positive recognition and feedback and how they can do better.

In the second conversation, you discuss *relative* outcomes. This is where you discuss how the individual's performance ranking is affected by judgements you have made about:

- changes in the competitive/operating environment
- observed degree of difficulty of various people's goals

---

[9] You don't have to use A/B/C ratings of course — some might argue that a B grade is demotivating for high performers given its school grade associations. 'R' for 'Role Model', 'L' for 'Lives the Values', and 'I' for 'Issues to discuss' work fine — but I personally prefer to grab people's attention with an A or a C.

- relative importance to the organisation of different contributions
- relative performance against competitors over the same period
- extraordinary contributions from individuals beyond their own goals
- extraordinary problems or risk issues that emerged outside of agreed goals.

By being clear on the difference between rating and ranking, you acknowledge the hard work by the individual and their achievements but make no excuses for your role as a leader in using judgement to assess relative performance.

Top performers can gain pride in their relative achievements, and the obstacles they've overcome. Low performers may not *like* your judgement, and may still disagree with where they are ranked, but retain pride in what they've accomplished and are more likely to accept that the system is broadly fair.

Note that this combination of absolute and relative performance discussions also helps protect against the possibility that people who are simply good at negotiating lower targets look better than those who deliberately take on tougher assignments.

Relative performance discussions also benefit from the discipline of 'calibration' sessions at the end of a performance period, before individual discussions take place. In these sessions, leaders meet with their peer leaders to debate proposed ratings and rankings of their collective subordinates in a meeting overseen by their boss. This can be a time-consuming and confronting process, but it helps build a common understanding of what good looks like in an organisation. It also helps weaker leaders gain the insight and courage to tackle difficult issues — for example, where a team member's behaviour with peers isn't visible to their immediate manager.

Consequences

The final aspect of a good review process is about consequence.

Positive consequences are easy — everyone likes to deliver good news. But without clear consequences for failure, the value of Clarity will fall, along with engagement.

The reality is that many leaders — even some at the very top of large companies — dislike conflict so much that they sometimes tolerate consistent failure of behaviour or delivery rather than taking action that will bring them into conflict with someone they know and like. It's a common mistake — but one with serious consequences.

Where values or behavioural standards are breached, a bad apple really does spoil the whole barrel. What is 'normal' can change quickly if poor behaviour isn't addressed. Consequences for breaches of this sort need to be swift and public, leaving no doubt about your commitment as a leader to upholding the values. Depending on the seriousness of the breach, this can range from public censure, formal written warnings or termination.

Goal failures require leaders to exercise more judgement: in a growth mindset, some level of failure should be welcomed if people are stretching themselves. However, leaders should be clear that consistent mistakes or failure to deliver on things that were eminently achievable do not get rewarded with endless chances and new career opportunities. And if this is made clear enough, I've found that people who aren't meeting the mark on either values or delivery will often recognise the fact and leave of their own accord.

How to know if it's working

True Clarity in an organisation will manifest itself in a number of ways beyond higher engagement scores.

If roles are clear:

- things will get done faster
- meetings will require fewer people
- decisions will 'stick' rather than being overturned by people with different perspectives or perceived authority.

On the other hand, 'dropped balls' on projects or safety, risk or compliance obligations are signs that people are not clear enough about their job roles and accountabilities.

If goals are clear, both from a lead and lag perspective, teams will work effectively together and rapidly build a track record of small wins that add up to significant delivery and advancement. A strong and efficient operating rhythm will be in place. Meetings will also be shorter and focused on issue resolution and coordination rather than endless 'first principles' debates that sometimes characterise team meetings.

And if behaviour expectations are clear, the language and stories in the organisation will become more consistent. Rather than simply existing in a dusty document, the values become a source of pride and reference point for 'the way things are done around here' and 'the way we make decisions'. Great people will be knocking on the door to join, seeing the values as aligned to their own. High performers will be consistently targeted by the competition, but won't want to leave because they feel at home and supported in the organisation's culture.

It's also worth noting that Clarity also makes your job easier: it's easier to see what is being done well, and what isn't. It's easier to spot those who are performing well. And it's easier to coach those who are falling behind.

CLARITY

Summary

Clarity is the backbone of engagement. Almost everyone wants to be and feel successful at work, but many leaders assume that what success looks like is obvious. Often, it isn't.

Leaders need to make sure that each individual:

- understands and is qualified for their role
- is involved in setting their own stretch targets
- knows what lead measures they should be focused on
- knows what behaviour is expected of them in order to live the organisation's values.

This needs to be followed up with ongoing formal and informal feedback so that a true growth mindset can take hold.

When combined with genuine Care and meaningful Context, Clarity puts a leader and an organisation well on the way to high engagement.

In the next two chapters we'll examine the aspects of the Leadership Star that make that success sustainable.

Questions for reflection

1. Role Clarity
   - Does each team member have a clear job description in place that you've reviewed together?
   - Are the various roles across the organisation clear enough in terms of their accountabilities and overlap?
   - Are people sufficiently empowered to deliver in their roles?

2. Goal Clarity
   - Does each individual have a clear performance document with an appropriate number of goals?
   - Have stretch targets been defined with the individual's input?
   - Have clear lead and lag indicators been identified, with tracking established?
   - Are the consequences of missing goals understood?

3. Behavioural Clarity
   - Are the organisation's values clearly defined?
   - Has the relevant behaviour (what's okay and what isn't) for each value been documented and agreed with the team?
   - Is behavioural assessment formally incorporated into the review process?

4. Feedback process
   - Are regular feedback sessions on progress scheduled?
   - Are you highlighting and helping people build on their strengths?
   - Are the consequences of missing goals clearly understood?
   - Are the consequences of poor behaviour clear and publicised?

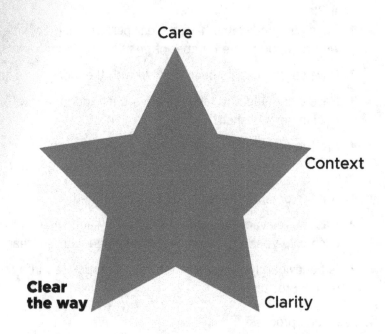

CLEAR THE WAY

Nearly a hundred people sauntered into the operations centre's cafeteria for my first presentation as the new managing director of the bank's credit card business. Some sat politely in plastic chairs around the lunch tables. Others stood just outside the lunchroom, leaning on the filing cabinets that defined the borders of the breakout area.

A few company veterans, grey-haired and -bearded, stood at the back of the room, arms folded. Their body language made it clear that they had heard it all before. I was conscious that my dark blue suit and tie stood out in a room full of casually dressed people (with the exception of the veterans, who wore the company tie over their short-sleeved shirts).

I was nervous, but confident that they would soon be as excited as I was about the future.

I launched into my presentation, running through my full-colour PowerPoint slides. I showed how our business was performing versus the competition, talked up the growth in online sales and committed to building a world-class, high-performing culture.

After about 20 minutes, having (I thought) dazzled them with my strategic insights, I smiled in what I thought was my most engaging way, and wrapped up.

'Okay! Let's open it up,' I said. 'Who has questions?'

Silence.

A hundred pairs of eyes stared back at me. The women in the plastic seats looked up pleasantly, and then back down at their feet. The young men behind the filing cabinets shifted nervously, leaning from one arm to another. The veterans at the back of the room just stared blankly, arms still folded.

More silence.

'Okay, surely you must have some questions?' I said. 'Ask me about anything!'

Another very long pause. It became embarrassingly clear I wasn't going anywhere until someone asked a question.

Finally, a young man in the back corner slowly started to raise his hand. Before he had it fully raised, I was onto him.

'Yes — great — a question. What would you like to know?' I was sure that this would finally be the icebreaker on an interesting discussion about our strategy and priorities.

My questioner looked a bit nervous, if not downright sheepish.

'Um, could we get a new copy machine?' There was a murmur in the crowd — the first noise anyone had made.

'A new *copy machine*?' I asked. This was not what I was expecting to talk about. 'Tell me more.'

'Well, the copy machine we use breaks down all the time. So we're constantly standing in a queue waiting for someone to fix it.'

'Do you use the copy machine a lot?' I asked.

'Yes — it's part of every file that we work. We have to copy the contract for the file and send the other one to the customer.'[1]

I paused for a moment. This seemed a pretty simple fix.

'Okay, let's get a new copy machine,' I said, with a somewhat puzzled shrug.

---

[1] This took place in 1999 — the pre-digital dark ages for most bank operations!

The room broke out into applause. All of a sudden, even the wizened veterans at the back had dropped their folded arms and were whispering to each other.

'Can I ask *you* a question?' I said, looking back at my questioner. 'Why didn't you just get a new copier before? Why did you need to ask me?'

'Well, management said we don't have budget for it.'

'What?!?' I said. 'But that's silly — we'd be wasting a lot more cost having everyone standing around in a queue, surely.'

His shrug and raised eyebrows told me everything I needed to know — there was an edgy conversation coming with my operations head.

'Okay, leave it with me.' I said. 'And if you have any more issues like this that are getting in the way, please email me directly and I'll get them fixed.'

Another round of applause!!

'Maybe this management gig isn't so hard after all,' I thought.[2]

This experience, early in my career as a manager, taught me one of the most important lessons about building engagement as a leader: it's your job to knock over barriers — to Clear the way — for your people.

If you've followed the steps in the first three chapters, you've shown your people that you Care about them as individuals, helped them see the Context and meaning in their work, and given them Clarity on what's expected of them. What remains is to help them achieve the goals that you've set.

Assuming you've hired well, most people will have the basic intent, aptitude and values needed to deliver what is asked of them — especially if they've been involved in setting those goals. So, in most cases, the job of the leader is to get out of the way and let people get on with it — to be a sounding board when needed, to check in on progress occasionally, but otherwise to intervene only when a course correction is needed.

But Clearing the way is one aspect of leadership where it's important to continue to be proactive. You have to explicitly ask, 'What's getting in

---

[2] How wrong I was!

the way?' You have to look with a critical eye at what's happening (and what isn't).

And then you need to take action.

What's blocking you?

Sometimes, like in my copy machine story, Clearing the way really is as simple as asking what's getting in the way and taking action on the suggestions that get raised. People may know exactly what they need, but for one reason or another are afraid to raise it with you.

In large organisations, people may have had a bad experience with a manager who essentially taught them not to stick their hand up.

This could be because the manager had a misguided desire to look confident in front of *their* boss, or a 'penny-wise, pound-foolish' approach to managing their budget. Perhaps the leader created the impression that some in their team were less important than others, and the 'second-class citizens' felt they would never get the resources they needed, so they stopped bothering to ask. This is particularly insidious in an organisation if it leads to a sense of learned helplessness — where people start seeing themselves as victims and stop taking initiative to overcome obstacles.

Sometimes leaders' lack of understanding may simply be from ignorance: for example, well-paid senior people may not realise the challenges that more junior people face in simply getting to work by public transport or meeting targets to a level that allows them to keep their job.

Other leaders may be afraid to ask their people about the constraints that they face, fearing either that they won't be able to fix it — thereby disappointing their people — or that they'll reveal their own ignorance, causing them to lose face or respect from their people.

Leaders also need to be aware of unintended consequences in how they ask for information. For example, saying 'don't bring me problems unless you can bring me a solution', while meant to empower people to be creative and proactive, can have the opposite effect of driving problems underground.

By contrast, the best leaders ask their people what's getting in the way, all the time — and show that they're genuinely interested by taking action and following up to fix the issue. As one CEO told me, 'Your capacity to reduce misery is much larger than you think.'

This doesn't mean you have to 'play Father Christmas' as a leader: sometimes there are genuine constraints that people have to deal with. But showing that you have a genuine interest in removing barriers will go a long a way towards demonstrating empathy and building your team's trust and engagement.

Identifying barriers

The most obvious way to identify barriers is to simply ask, 'what's in the way?' when in:

- team and project meetings, as a formal agenda item
- larger presentations and town hall meetings
- site visits, when chatting with individuals or small groups
- emails to individuals, team leaders and the broader organisation, inviting people to write back directly or via a confidential whistle-blower channel.

At Westpac, I made a tradition of giving a prize in every public forum — usually a bottle of champagne — to the person who asked me the curliest question or told me something I didn't want to hear.

Often the issues raised by people related to some form of constraint or barrier they were experiencing — giving me a chance to address the issue on the spot, or to 'turn the burner up a bit' under a leader who wasn't doing their job properly.

But aside from identifying issues to fix, the 'curly question' ritual helped me remind people that if they didn't speak up, leaders wouldn't necessarily know what was going on.

A similar approach is to make a point of 'owning the bad stuff': after reviewing all the comments from the staff engagement survey, one CEO I know makes a point of reading out the hardest comments in front of large company meetings: 'This one goes right into my heart!' he'll say, before talking about what he's going to personally do about it.

In a healthy, open culture, this tradition goes beyond the CEO: another organisation I know holds regular 'Feedback Friday' or 'What's up Wednesday' events, where each leader sends out emails to around 20 hand-picked staff, asking two simple questions: 'What's in your way when serving clients?' and 'What's in the way of clients doing more business with us?'

Who you ask matters: don't just ask people one or two levels down the chain of command. The best insights often come from junior people at the coalface, especially people who are too new to the organisation to take the current state of play for granted.

To broaden the reach for feedback, some organisations set up 'easy to do business with' mailboxes, with teams and resources dedicated to prioritising and fixing the suggestions that come in, no matter how small.

Given some people may be reluctant to complain, it can also be helpful to ask outsiders who interact with your people about what they see as your constraints. For example, service providers, vendors, union officials and especially customers themselves may see things more clearly than people who are 'in the dance' every day.

When you start actively soliciting feedback you may find that the number and scope of suggestions or complaints becomes overwhelming. Some leaders get frustrated when the 'barriers' people mention seem frivolous, or people have unrealistic expectations. I'd encourage you to keep at it: 'Look for the gold', as one CEO I know likes to describe it.

Instead of looking to hear *your* priorities played back to you, try to work out what people really care about — safety in the workplace, the quality of their tools, or fairness in how people are treated, for example. You might find you can do something about these broader themes that really makes a difference.

Go and look!

Despite a leader's best efforts to solicit them, not every barrier or constraint is going to be raised by people in answer to a question. You have to use your experience and critical perspective to go looking for them as well: learn with your eyes!

Talk to customers

The best starting point is to talk to customers — particularly those who have complained. Verbatim feedback from complaints can often highlight process or policy issues that are getting in the way of providing good service, and therefore almost certainly frustrating the staff as well.

While printed reports on complaints data are valuable, meeting in person with affected customers is a great way both to repair relationships and to identify subtle issues that may be getting in the way for staff. This is because complaints data and customer experiences are almost always 'shaded' in some way as they pass up the chain.

While direct interactions can be confronting, and some customer perspectives need to be taken with a grain of salt, it's remarkable how often a terrible customer experience — when explored directly by a more senior person — can lead to deeper insights about what is and isn't working in the organisation.

For example, meetings like this have often helped me identify:

- outdated policies that no-one thought to challenge
- systems that weren't working as promised
- parts of the organisation that weren't coordinating with each other.

Talk to front-line staff

One bank CEO I know makes a point, when visiting branches, of not just asking people what they're working on, but asking them to *show him* what they're doing. 'Show me the form you use ... show me the screen you look at. No, really — *show me!*' He might then follow up with 'How long does that take? Why so long ... who are you waiting for?' And he's not averse to pulling out his phone on the spot and ringing the department head in question to ask why it takes *them* so long to respond to the branch staff.

While the branch member on the receiving end of this interrogation often starts out feeling decidedly nervous, they soon work out what the CEO's doing: he's looking for ways to clear the way for *them*. Needless to say, this CEO makes many people in operations, credit and technology nervous — but he is *loved* by his branch staff.

Similar opportunities can often be identified through business or operational reviews, project deep dives and 'skip-level' meetings (with the direct reports of your direct reports). To get people to open up in these sessions, it's important to create the right atmosphere up front. Tell people why you're doing it. As one CEO I know of tells his people:

> *When you're CEO sometimes your people only tell you things you want to hear. In great companies that's not true, but we aren't a great culture company yet. So I try to explain when I ask front-line employees how it's going — this isn't about criticising your bosses — I'm not going to run back to your manager and say so and so has a negative attitude. What I will do is after speaking to many people I will aggregate the themes, and if I see a theme emerging then I'll ask my leadership team to dive in deeper. My promise to you, the employee, is that if you're honest with me, everything you say I will only use for good.*

Talk to third parties

It can also be revealing to ask vendors, business partners and consultants for their perspective on what's getting in the way of your people's success. These suggestions need to be taken with a pinch of salt — make sure you look at the evidence, time frames and results that people are sharing, and ask yourself whether they make sense or not.

Ask the stupid questions

Finally, don't be afraid to ask stupid questions.[3] Ask people to explain, in detail:

- How does the process work?
- Who else is involved, and who does what exactly?
- Why do you do it that way?[4]

---

[3] One of the best career decisions I made years ago was a commitment to always ask stupid questions. It demonstrates self-confidence, helps you learn how things work in detail, and there's often someone else in the room who has the same question but is too shy to ask!

[4] This is also a great opportunity to use the 'five whys' approach from Six Sigma reengineering: Asking 'why' about an issue, and then continuing to ask 'why' again until the true root cause of an issue is identified.

- How long does it take?

- What results are you getting?

- What are the exceptions?

- What problems and bottlenecks are you encountering?

- How are you overcoming them?

- What's getting in the way?

- Is there anything I or my team can do to help?

These questions will often lead you to identify barriers or constraints that the individual hadn't even considered — for example, incorrectly assuming that some other part of the organisation has to be consulted before a decision was made.

I once asked an operations team, 'How often does the product team say no to your recommendation?' as they explained how a particular customer process worked. 'Oh, never,' was the answer. 'So why send it to them at all?' I asked. (We changed the process, thereby accelerating customer responses by an average of two weeks.)

Being seen to take notes and sending a follow-up message after visits like these is a powerful tactic that quickly echoes through the team you visited, since it shows you are taking them and their insights seriously. It doesn't have to be a long note — simply thank them for their time, summarise what you heard and comment on what you plan to do with their insights.

Clear the way through 'Session D'

Another approach that can be effective in helping people to clear the way — particularly on projects — is what I call the 'Session D' approach.[5]

---

[5] 'Session D' is based on an approach I learned from Ram Charan, the globally renowned author and consultant to some of the world's largest companies and most successful CEOs.

In Session D — the 'D' stands for Details and Decisions — project leaders give an open-ended presentation on their project to the entire senior team, highlighting the challenges that they are facing and the decisions that they need to make so that the senior team can help clear the way for the project.

Unlike a normal project review, this session has a number of important ground rules:

- All members of the most senior team with decision-making authority over any aspect of the project's dependencies or impacts *must* attend.

- Presentations are led by the day-to-day project leader, not just the senior sponsor.

- No questions or interruptions are allowed during the initial presentation, other than points of clarification, for example, 'I'm sorry, but I don't understand that — can you please explain it again.'

- There is no time limit on the presentation.

The presenters are asked to follow a very specific format:

- Presenters give an overview of their project, including:
    - what problem they're trying to solve
    - how they're approaching it, and why
    - what choices they've made on key design issues
    - what key decisions they've made
    - what resource or constraint issues they're facing
    - what support they need from other parts of the organisation
    - what key decisions they have coming up.

- No formal PowerPoint presentation is allowed: the presenters must simply talk (from notes, if needed) about the issues listed.

- A few key exhibits and detailed graphs or illustrations (including by slide) are encouraged, but only if they bring to life the details of the issues being discussed.

- Presenters are told to take as long as they want to tell their story and assured that they won't be interrupted.

Once the initial presentation is complete, then — and only then — the senior people begin to question the team. However, the style of questioning should be supportive rather than critical, focused on identifying areas where the senior team can clear the way for the project, for example, by:

- allocating needed people or financial resources
- giving direction on design or supplier choices
- cutting through bureaucratic logjams
- accelerating key decisions.

Senior people are encouraged to share their experience and state their opinions on important design choices or decisions, but the chair of the meeting — usually the CEO or relevant business head — needs to ensure that any decision to over-rule the project team is clearly justified based on facts or experience.

Similarly, any disputes must be properly aired and resolved in the room and then decisions must be accepted by all parties — the goal is to avoid people relitigating disputes outside the meeting.

The 'Clear the way' benefit comes from having all the key decision makers in the room *and* giving the team time to fully explain their approach and thinking without the senior interruptions that often occur in a typical meeting. In this way senior people develop a more nuanced understanding of the problems and key decision points, while still bringing their experience and seniority to bear in ways that accelerate the project.

The *tone* of the meeting is important for this approach to help rather than harm engagement: having to present without slides to the most senior people in the organisation can be stressful and intimidating, particularly if things aren't going well or uncomfortable truths need to be raised. Before the meeting starts, senior people are reminded to ask their questions in a supportive, exploratory way, rather than being overtly critical, dismissive or demeaning.

This commitment is important, because if the senior people go on the attack or aren't seen to behave in a collaborative and supportive way, employees quickly learn to avoid these sessions and think twice before raising their concerns. For this reason it's worth having a neutral advisor—a senior executive from another part of the organisation, say, or a trusted outside consultant—participate or even chair the session to make sure it stays on track and any poor or inconsiderate behaviour is addressed quickly.

While the Session D approach may seem overly structured, it's remarkably effective.

The first time we used it, my leadership team developed a much greater understanding of one of our major investments and the role they and their teams each had in making it successful: in a number of cases, junior members of their team hadn't highlighted the ways in which other teams were depending on them.

When I asked—towards the end of a three-plus-hour meeting—what decisions were coming up, we discovered that we could resolve on the spot an issue the project team was planning to spend the next six weeks analysing, thanks to the specific experience of one senior leader. This one decision both accelerated the project significantly and reduced the project spend.

Too much detail?

Some leaders may take the view that it isn't their job to get into this much detail. 'I'm too busy,' they might say. 'I need to be thinking at a more strategic level, and that's what my direct reports are for.'

While I'm all for empowerment and delegation, there's an important subtlety here. Diving into the detail is not about doing everyone's job for them. It's about recognising that, as a leader, you bring experience and a broader perspective to what happens in the organisation that can add value to your people.

When you choose to 'dive in' to understand and clear the barriers, you are showing that you appreciate their efforts, want them to succeed, and see your role as being there to help. You also set a good example for other leaders about how you expect them to lead *their* people.

'Diving in' doesn't mean you can—or should—try to have all the answers. When tackling engagement issues, for example, it can be much more powerful to put a team of high performers on the hook to understand and fix issues. They are more likely to identify the issues' root causes anyway, and the broader organisation will take confidence from knowing that teams of their peers have been assigned to address the issues.

Done in this spirit, 'diving in' will empower — not disempower — your team, thereby helping drive engagement.

When NOT to clear the way

There is one important caveat: sometimes it's best to *not* clear the way. Constraints — and pressure — can be valuable!

This is particularly true when innovative solutions are required, or the organisation is subject to genuine constraints.

Constraints — deadlines, budgets, geographic limits, access to particular people or resources, or the need to comply with specific regulations — can accelerate progress by helping people break out of mental boxes that limit creativity.

Apple, Amazon, Microsoft, Dell and even Disney are all examples of companies that were started on a shoestring in a garage. Steve Jobs famously limited Apple's engineers to only four products when he came back to save the company in 1997. Discount airlines began to thrive when they set the goal of being cheaper than car or train travel. Amazon's Jeff Bezos is famous for his 'two pizza' rule that limits how large a project team can be.

Constraints that limit choice make it easier for people to make decisions and move forward: psychological studies have demonstrated that too much choice creates stress and works against rapid decision making.[6] In a business planning or project management context, unbounded possibilities can easily lead to analysis paralysis.

---

[6] See for example, 'Choice overload reduces neural signatures of choice set value in dorsal striatum and anterior cingulate cortex' by Elena Reutskaja et al., *Nature Human Behaviour*, October 2018.

'How unreasonable should I be?' is a common judgement challenge for leaders. And while I've never found a simple answer to this question, I do have a few observations.

First, make sure you are clear on what the real constraints are, and communicate them to your team. If there's a genuine cash flow, competitive or regulatory constraint, don't shy away from explaining what must be done.

Second, use stretch thinking to set artificial constraints. For example, if you give people a month to analyse a key decision, are they really going to get a better answer than if they only have a week? (Agile software development and project management uses constraints such as this to great effect.)

Third, experience suggests that you can almost always be more unreasonable than you think. As an experienced leader, your understanding of how things have been done in the past, and your judgement on what is possible, may limit your perception of what your team can achieve — so don't be afraid to ask your people for more. They may surprise you.

Among the managers who shaped *my* career, the ones I most respect — the ones who taught me what 'good' looked like — were often the most unreasonable. They set ridiculous deadlines, and often threw me in way over my head to deal with issues about which I had no experience. Some were flat-out obnoxious.

Did I learn a lot from working with them? Absolutely — those experiences were essential to my development. Did I enjoy working for them? Occasionally. Did it make me feel highly engaged? Sometimes: where I perceived that, deep down, they were genuinely interested in helping me and believed I could do better, I was willing to put up with a lot (and some of the most difficult bosses are now dear friends, decades later). In contrast, I was happy to see the back of the ones that treated me as a disposable resource.

That leads me to the final point to share about Clearing the way: look out for a wide range of potential barriers and constraints, not all of which are visible.

Physical barriers

Physical working environments rightly get a lot of attention in discussions on engagement. Potential engagement-killers to watch out for include:

- inconvenient locations (hard to get to through public or private transport)

- safety concerns (due to poor location or lack of security measures/procedures)

- unhealthy workspaces (due to lack of social distancing, poor heating/ac/ventilation, or unsanitary kitchen/toilet facilities)

- lack of access to amenities such as food, coffee, exercise or childcare facilities

- poor lighting, workspace ergonomics or building layouts

- lack of privacy or areas to concentrate

- lack of suitable spaces for breaks, team meetings, or after-work socialising

- inadequate tools, technology and equipment (for example, the copy machine story!).

Note that relative changes in these areas can particularly hurt engagement—one company I know saw a huge morale drop when they shrunk the size of cubicles allocated to people in pursuit of a small property cost saving.

On the positive side, a good working environment can be a big advantage in both recruitment and engagement: who wouldn't want to work in a modern building, with a nice view, good coffee, a gym, a comfortable desk and breakout spaces?

However, there are several subtleties worth bearing in mind when investing in new offices.

First, a workspace that looks good doesn't necessarily work well. I've seen many offices that have won design awards but are full of chairs you can't sit on, much less work in.

Second, the space sends an important signal to the staff about the values of the organisation. A retailer who claims to be committed to everyday low prices sends a very different message to staff if senior leaders eat their lunch in a catered dining room.

And finally, a good space will never make up for a bad manager. Some of the most engaged branch teams I've met worked in run-down sites that dated from the 1970s, while some of the least engaged drone away in brand-new facilities.

Identifying and clearing small barriers that your people contend with every day is a great way to show them you care and goes a long way to building engagement.

The best office refurbishment programs set as their first design principle that 'staff need to love working here'. With input from staff surveys and focus groups, I've seen this principle lead to small but important inclusions such as dishwashers for the staff room, lockable cupboards for handbags, coffee machines, refrigerators, 'honour bars' for healthy snacks and drinks, and even a choice of chair for each staff member. Finding ways for people to customise their environment (through choice of paint, furnishings, technology or decoration) can also go a long way towards boosting engagement.

In modern offices, amenities such as subsidised internal cafés, breastfeeding rooms, prayer rooms, gym and yoga rooms, free annual flu shots, and dedicated rooms for physiotherapy and massage can make a big difference to engagement, both by boosting productivity (fewer reasons to leave work!) and by imputing a sense that the organisation cares about the employees' overall wellbeing.

A related—but often debated—topic is whether companies should provide free food, coffee and so on to employees, or whether this breeds an inefficient, 'entitled' atmosphere.

An obvious consideration is the extent to which such elements are standard in a given industry. (I've lost track of how many kombucha kegs I've seen at Silicon Valley startups!) Anecdotally, if perks are overdone and not coupled with strong performance disciplines, they can undermine a productive culture.

On the other hand, I've seen examples where relatively low-cost benefits such as free breakfasts or soft drinks are cited as key contributors to some companies' highly engaged cultures.

The answer is most likely about alignment with the company's values and business strategy: free massages and a flash new building environment hardly send a message about cost control to a low-cost retailer's staff, while providing single-ply toilet paper certainly doesn't gel with a 'we care about you' message to a few thousand retail branch staff!

Similar care should be devoted to thinking about the tools that are provided to specialist staff in performing their roles. Outdated or under-powered technology, machinery or systems that constantly break down, or lack of access to important data sets or online tools can quickly demotivate high-performing specialists. By contrast, access to state-of-the-art tools can be a great motivator for people who aspire to be the best in their chosen discipline.

Financial barriers

Most organisations have financial constraints that become real or perceived barriers to what people can do. These can become demotivating if they are too far out of sync with the goals that have been set. Budget constraints on spending are the most common example, but in a commercial organisation most aspects of the P&L and balance sheet of a business can turn into constraints, for example through:

- market commitments on revenue or sales growth
- minimum margin hurdles or return on capital limits
- assumptions on loss rates, amortisation or shrinkage
- required maintenance or contracted cost increases
- mandatory investment allocations
- maximum borrowing or balance sheet structuring limits.

Although many of these constraints are real, good leaders encourage their people to identify and challenge those assumptions — since often only the leaders themselves can change them.

Sometimes this discussion can force leaders to rethink and refocus their stated priorities, including stopping projects that are 'nice to have' but getting in the way of more important initiatives.

Similarly, the open discussion of constraints often leads to more nuanced understanding of the rationale for those constraints and more creative thinking about what trade-offs are possible.

Some of the most powerful constraints are so embedded in 'the way we do things around here' that no-one thinks to question them. I call assumptions such as these 'prisons of the mind'.

A classic 'prison of the mind' is the requirement that 'thou shalt not give up revenue'.

During financial target setting, managers typically require every business and product to plan on growing its revenue line. The unintended consequence of this is that people assume that they can't possibly give up revenue from an existing product or revenue source — since to do so would just make their current challenge harder.

In banks, one consequence of this assumption was a proliferation of new products, features and fees as managers sought new sources of revenue to add on top of what they already had. This in turn created enormous business and technical complexity—leading to cost and servicing issues — as well as reputation issues when products or business arrangements no longer met customer or community expectations.

Assumptions such as these are a great opportunity to clear the way: by identifying unwritten financial assumptions such as 'never give up revenue', leaders can make it clear to their people that, for example, 'I *will* give up current period revenue if it makes our business more sustainable for the long term'. Once people believe that everything is on the table, they are more likely to think creatively and identify solutions that build long-term value — and to feel more supported and engaged as a result.

A related barrier can develop through insufficient or unclear authority— to authorise spending, to appoint qualified people, to make design decisions or to sign agreements and make implementation commitments.

Each organisation has its own philosophy around how much oversight or signoff is required at different levels in the organisation. But intervening to make these processes work better—building a culture where bureaucratic 'veto rights' are few and far between — is an important role for leaders. Clarifying who has the right to decide versus the right to be consulted can make a big difference to the speed of action and the feeling of empowerment needed for engagement.[7]

Invisible barriers

A genuine commitment to Clear the way means proactively looking for anything that gets in the way of people achieving their goals and targets.

Barriers such as the working environment, tools, financial resources and decision authority are relatively straightforward to identify. However, there are several subtler categories of potential barriers that leaders should watch out for:

- intellectual
- cultural
- emotional
- political.

Intellectual barriers

Intellectual barriers arise where people:

- haven't had the appropriate training for their role
- lack sufficient experience in the area (for example, they don't understand the needs and thought patterns of a target customer segment or important group of business partners)
- lack the intellectual capacity to handle the job requirements.

While some people will happily acknowledge they need more training, for many the fear of losing face or 'imposter syndrome' will keep them grinding away in silent fear of being found out.

---

[7] For a discussion on how to address this, see 'Who has the D: How clear decision roles enhance organizational performance' by Paul Rogers and Marcia W. Blenko, *Harvard Business Review*, January 2006.

Cultural barriers

Cultural barriers can arise in a number of ways. Aside from literal differences in culture — such as, language, accent or behavioural variations across geographies, religions or nationalities — cultural barriers can also arise across divides in age, gender, socio-economic, demographic, sexual preference and even political beliefs.

Team diversity can and should be a great strength — my experience is that diverse thinking leads to better judgement and decision making. However, from an engagement point of view diversity brings three key risks.

First, cultural differences can make it harder for people to communicate and therefore get things done. Second, differences in expectations around acceptable behaviour (including humour) can get in the way of building the relationship bonds that underpin a highly engaged team. And third, culture differences can lead individuals in the minority to feel ostracised or even bullied — which is engagement kryptonite.

To avoid these risks, a central role of good leadership is to make everyone feel valued and welcome.

The negative halo of a culturally insensitive leader is a sure drag on engagement (and, most likely, on performance as well). Whereas a leader who shows through their actions that they value diversity, encourages their people to 'bring their whole selves to work' and doesn't tolerate discrimination or bullying is directly clearing the way for everyone to be their best.

Emotional barriers

Another category to watch out for is emotional barriers. Studies[8] show that, far from being strictly rational beings, most people make their decisions from an emotional basis, which they then rationalise after the fact. This means that insecurity, fear, anxiety, anger, ambition, resentment, jealousy, pride and so on are almost always underneath

---

[8] See for example, 'Emotion and decision making', by Jennifer S. Lerner, Ye Li, Piercarlo Valdesolo and Karim S. Kassam, *Annual Review of Psychology*, January 2015.

how people act at work and how engaged they feel in the work of the organisation.

For example, I once worked with an executive who had been fired from her previous job. Her error was inadvertent, but because she hadn't paid close enough attention to the terms of a supplier contract, her previous organisation had lost a lot of money when the supplier went bust. Her new job involved similar supplier oversight, but she was driving her staff crazy by nitpicking their work and dragging her feet on signing off new contracts.

The solution had two aspects to it — first, the executive had to recognise that her underlying fear of losing her job was causing a perpetual over-reaction and inability to move forward. And secondly, her team needed to understand the consequences of getting things wrong — which came when the executive opened up and shared her story with them.

As a leader, you have a coaching role to help your people to identify and overcome these emotional barriers — to help them 'be all that they can be'.

Political barriers

Political barriers feature in most large organisations. How often have you heard people at work complain about office politics?

Sometimes 'politics' derives from overlapping or conflicting objectives among different parts of the organisation, or a constraint on the resources needed to achieve those objectives. This is particularly true when there is conflict among the leader's own team: without genuine trust, alignment and collaboration among the most senior leaders, political conflict can rapidly cascade through the organisation.

When this occurs, it's up to the leader to help identify and reconcile the conflict — either by working through the issues within their own team, or, when the conflict is with another part of the organisation, by escalating to a level where sensible choices can be made.

At other times, the leader's public endorsement of a more junior person's project — or a polite request to a senior colleague for assistance — may be all that's needed to break through roadblocks.

If you believed television portrayals of corporate life, you might conclude that everyone is out to (metaphorically) stab each other in the back in order to get what they want. This perception often permeates large companies, and some leaders do deliberately set out to create conflict and competition among their people.

While 'survival of the fittest' *might* be a valid strategy at certain investment banks or law firms (although in the long run I doubt that), it works directly against the trusting relationships needed to sustain a high-engagement culture.

This internal competition assumption needs to be rooted out if you want to build engagement — and, frankly, it's usually wrong anyway. Human beings are quick to judge other people's motives, but our inbuilt biases have been shown to make us very bad at actually knowing why others do things.[9]

While there *are* examples of people who deliberately set out to undermine others, start with the premise that most people see themselves as 'the good guy' in the film that they're starring in. Similarly, it's generally safe to assume that people are behaving rationally *within their own context*.

A better assumption, when someone complains about a colleague's 'political' behaviour, is to assume that *everyone* is insecure. Once you do that, their 'political' behaviour will probably make sense.

In other words, help people to see that their colleagues are acting out of their *own* specific fears, insecurities and perceived constraints — rather than setting out to undermine others.

A similar assumption that can help defuse confrontations between colleagues:

'Everyone is suffering!'

This might sound melodramatic, but when things get heated there is almost always some underlying hurt that drives the perceived over-reaction.

Years ago, I worked with a polished and polite executive who looked and behaved like the successful executive from central

---

[9] See for example, elsevier.com, '5 pitfalls to understanding people's motives'.

casting — well-mannered, -groomed and fit, well-tailored suits, discreet but expensive car. But every so often, he would lash out aggressively whenever someone challenged his authority or the scope of his business. People would walk away burned by the experience, convinced that he was a power-hungry political animal.

As I got to know him better, and understand his personal history, it all became a bit clearer. He was from a broken home in a working-class suburb, and his mother had left him and his father. The father had gone bankrupt, and he had been pulled out of school to work at 16. Through his own hard work and dedication, he had scrambled up the corporate ladder and achieved a level of career and financial success. But lingering in the background was a fear that it could all be taken away. In our discussions I made it clear that his behaviour to his colleagues wasn't acceptable, and that, while I had sympathy for his hot buttons, he needed to learn to manage his 'stuff'. Thankfully, he agreed, and with the help of a coach was able to make great progress and repair most of the relationships with his peers.

As a team leader, encourage your team members to empathise with different styles and backgrounds, to look for the concerns and psychological 'stuff' that each of their colleagues is dealing with and to bring a generosity of spirit to resolving conflict. Likewise, be careful about how you react to mistakes; in a healthy culture, mistakes are welcomed as a powerful tool for learning rather than something to be punished.

At a one-on-one level, try to understand what makes each of your team members tick. This means understanding their:

- past successes and failures
- working style
- family situation and history

and anything else that colours their view of the world. With this sort of understanding, you are much more able to identify the sorts of hang-ups that may be holding people back — and be in a position to help clear them away.

If you pay attention, you'll start to spot common patterns: the young person who is over-confident and won't admit mistakes; the highly accomplished woman who never feels she's good enough to take on the next challenge; the rising 'whiz kid' who thinks his brilliance makes up for a lack of interest in people; the mid-career man who is so afraid of losing his job that any change is met with aggressive stone-walling. If you can figure out what's going on inside someone's head — and why — you have a chance to make a real difference to both them and your organisation.

Not every leader is skilled at this, so providing access to external coaching is another useful technique. Coaching styles and skills vary widely, so it's worth taking the time to find the right fit. But when combined with rigorous 360-degree feedback, a good coach can be very effective at helping people identify and clear their emotional barriers.

You might think that playing armchair psychologist is beyond the role of a leader managing grown adults, but it can make a real difference in helping your direct reports to gel in a way that builds both high engagement and strong results.

CLEAR THE WAY

Summary

To be engaged, people need to feel that that they are contributing to meaningful work, that they can be successful, and that they are growing as a person and in their career.

Any number of physical, financial or invisible barriers can get in the way of your people's success. While some people will put up their hand and ask for help, many others won't. Some won't even be aware of the barriers that they're facing—or that the perceived barrier is merely a 'prison of the mind'.

Clearing the way is an important role for leaders. To do it well, you need to be curious, you need to be proactive and you need to follow up—to demonstrate through your actions that you really do want to see your people succeed. You also need to devote real time to it. One colleague of mine describes this as the 'inverted pyramid': rather than the leader standing at the top, supported by all of his or her people, the leader's job is to be at the bottom of the pyramid, helping everyone to be their most successful self.[10]

To know *where* you need to intervene, it doesn't hurt to take a keen interest in your people's psychology—understanding what makes them tick. Which is another way of reinforcing the importance of the first C—Care. Coincidentally, these insights are also essential for making the most of the last of the five Cs—Celebrate—which we turn to in the next chapter.

---

[10] For a broader discussion on this idea, see *Servant Leadership: A journey into the nature of legitimate power and greatness*, by Robert K. Greenleaf.

Questions for reflection

- When is the last time you asked your people 'what's in the way'?

- How much time do you devote to really listening to your people?

- How do you get feedback from customers, business partners and outside vendors?

- What physical barriers or constraints do your people face in the workplace?

- Do they have the tools needed to succeed? How do you know?

- What unwritten financial assumptions might be holding people back?

- What legitimate constraints exist or should be imposed?

- How can we simplify to make things easier?

- What are the gaps in training, capability or needed authority for your people? How do you know?

- Do you know what makes each of your people tick? What hang-ups or baggage do they have that are getting in the way? How can you help them overcome it?

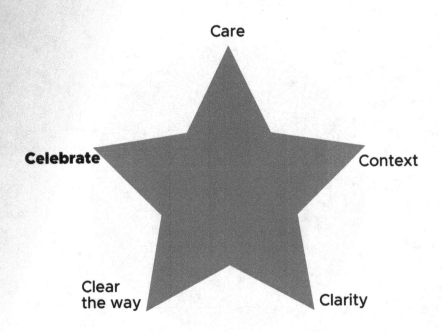

5

CELEBRATE

The hand-written letter started like many others I've received over the years:

'Dear Mr Hartzer,' I read aloud. 'I'm writing to thank you and draw to your attention the excellent service I've received from one of your staff.

'Over the past year,' the letter continued,

Jane Roberts has been enormously helpful in working through a number of complex financial issues, helping me sort out some of my loans, and even finding and clarifying issues around a number of my insurance policies, even though those policies aren't with your company.

'Pretty standard stuff,' I said, as I skimmed the letter. 'Nice to hear though.'

I kept reading:

She has done this on her own time, outside of normal working hours, without ever being asked. On a number of occasions, she has even called me in the evenings to remind me that I needed to do something and offered to swing by my home in the morning to pick up the paperwork.

'Wow, that's pretty dedicated,' I said. The letter continued:

She does all of this with a smile — nothing is ever too difficult, and she's been a great support to my wife and family as well. And the Easter basket of chocolate bunnies and Kinder Surprises for my kids really went down a treat.

'Easter basket?!' I exclaimed, looking up from the letter. 'That's serious dedication!'

And then the letter really grabbed my attention.

'I would be impressed by this level of service at any time,' the writer continued:

> But the fact that I have cancer, and only have another two or three months to live, means this help has added so much to my peace of mind as I try to sort as many things out as possible in advance for my family.
>
> Mr Hartzer, Westpac should be very proud to have someone like Jane Roberts on your staff, and I wanted to make sure that the contribution she has made to me and my family is properly recognised at the highest levels of the bank.
>
> Sincerely, David Austin[1]

The applause was thunderous.

The 300 people in the town hall meeting rose to their feet and started clapping as I choked out the last sentence. I'd read the letter many times by then, but reading it out loud in public, in front of Jane and all of her peers, took every bit of my self-control (and even then, it was touch and go ...).

Jane stayed in her seat, smiling (and crying) at the same time.

After allowing the applause to go on for a while, I asked Jane to join me on the stage.

'Jane,' I said,

> we're so incredibly proud of you. We talk a lot about service here — about helping — and that is one of the most amazing recognitions of service that I've seen.
>
> The fact that this man has decided to devote some of his short remaining time to writing a thank you letter to his bank is just amazing.
>
> You are an incredible role model, Jane, and you've reminded all of us here how much what we do matters to our customers. Thank you!

---

[1] Names and some details changed.

In response, Jane said a few humble words about what lovely people the Austins were, how sorry she felt for David and his family, how she was just pleased to be able to do something to help them.

(And knowing Jane, she meant it.)

There was another standing ovation as Jane sat down, beaming. When the meeting broke up Jane was mobbed by her peers — hugs and tears all around. As the audience went back to share Jane's story with their teams, you could see their chests puff with pride, a renewed sense of the difference that they and their teams could make in their customers' lives.

Building engagement isn't a one-off exercise. It's an ongoing process — a cycle that needs to be constantly reinforced.

If you demonstrate Care, share Context, provide Clarity and proactively Clear the way, chances are that your people will be successful, and their confidence will grow.

But to translate this success into sustainable engagement, you need to Celebrate. A lot.

By Celebrate, I don't just mean parties and award nights — although these have a role. And, as Jane's story shows, emotionally impactful recognition is seldom about money. Rather, it's about creating a culture of appreciation — making people feel valued by acknowledging the work they put in and the contribution they make, and rewarding them in ways that reinforce their commitment to the organisation and its overall purpose.

Recognition is one of those topics that, on the face of it, seems pretty straightforward. I'm sure you thank people for a job well done, and your organisation probably holds regular achievement awards and may even pay generous financial incentives.

These are good things — but for high engagement, recognition needs to be embedded in the culture and delivered in a wide variety of formal and informal ways.

Why recognition matters

When we celebrate achievement, we are associating pleasure with the 'pain' of the hard work and discipline it takes to achieve stretch goals. To our conscious — and unconscious — mind we are sending a message that yes, it's worth it. This builds resilience and commitment to continue in our efforts.

This principle can operate at two different levels:

- at a *conscious* level, chasing rewards of various kinds helps people commit to the effort required and stay motivated to overcome obstacles that get in the way

- at an *unconscious* level, celebration builds a positive association and meaning with work that might not otherwise be fun.

Without frequent recognition, people lose interest in applying discretionary effort and feel less loyalty to their employer — they disengage. A recent Gallup survey showed that employees who don't feel adequately recognised are twice as likely to say they'll quit over the next 12 months.[2] And high performers who don't feel recognised are also more likely to leave, since they have more options.

Meanwhile, a well-designed recognition program keeps the engagement wheel turning — reinforcing care, meaning, achievement and personal growth.

So, what are the elements of a highly engaging employee recognition program?

While the specifics will vary depending on the industry, economic challenges and personalities involved, an effective recognition program needs to cover several 'AND's:

- frequent AND periodic
- top down AND bottom up
- informal AND formal

---

[2] See gallup.com, 'Employee recognition: Low cost, high impact', by Annamarie Mann and Nate Dvorak.

- individual AND team
- focused AND fair.

Sound complicated? It doesn't have to be. But a list of considerations this long hopefully helps you recognise that celebrating effectively requires much more than Friday drinks and the annual 'all-star' awards dinner for top salespeople.

Let's look at each of these principles, along with some examples of how they can be implemented in practice.

Frequent AND periodic

To drive the engagement flywheel, continuous recognition needs to be embedded as a fundamental part of the organisation's culture. Relying on annual reviews and bonus conversations, or even semi-annual or quarterly discussions, puts too much time between an individual's day-to-day efforts and the psychic reinforcement that comes from regular praise and feedback.

A structured recognition program makes sure that the process happens and that every employee gets feedback on their performance and recognition for their personal contribution.

It's important that results are quickly celebrated or rewarded. This allows people to clearly link the rewards with their efforts for the year and puts them in a good frame of mind to set the next period's stretching targets. If there's too much of a gap between the outcome and the recognition, the two things become less tightly linked in people's minds, and the recognition loses its impact.

Beyond the annual or semi-annual cycle, a second level of periodic recognition is needed to create a positive feedback loop. This is generally done through regular performance check-ins between managers and their direct reports. For example, at Westpac Motivate goals are tracked centrally for each staff member, who then meets quarterly with their manager to review progress. In a less formal version, monthly 'Talk to me' meetings are held between each employee and their manager, using a one-page discussion template to review progress, highlight achievements and share feedback.

The outcomes of these reviews then filter up to a departmental or whole-of-business recognition program, with public celebration through town hall meetings or business-wide communications.

While these two separate recognition cycles are important, they're not sufficient.

What's *also* needed is a devotion to expressions of gratitude and informal recognition that are so embedded in employee behaviour that they become almost unconscious — Gallup research[3] suggests high engagement requires recognition to take place at least weekly.

The frequency is important — if you wait too long to recognise people, you lose the chance to link the positive feelings in the person's brain with the action that earned it. Plus, more frequent positive feedback creates a level of trust that makes people more likely to accept occasional constructive criticism later.

This culture of appreciation is more likely to emerge if senior leaders make a point of role-modelling frequent recognition. But it can also be helpful to embed this in standardised meeting agendas at various levels of the company.

For example, many of the best service companies, such as Ritz Carlton (and Westpac), hold structured 'service huddles' daily (or at least weekly) that start by recognising service anniversaries, key life events and career milestones among the members of each team. With practice and repetition, this rapidly becomes something that most staff — and not just the senior leaders — do instinctively.

Top down AND bottom up

There's no question that recognition from senior leaders is important. On field visits, I was often struck by the number of signed certificates I saw displayed proudly on walls, along with photographs of people

---

[3] See gallup.com, 'Employee recognition: Low cost, high impact', by Annamarie Mann and Nate Dvorak.

receiving awards from me or one of my predecessors. Similar pride was on display when people were called to the stage in town hall meetings by their divisional executive or invited to an annual 'night of nights' for high achievers.

Gallup surveys show that the most impactful recognition comes first from one's direct manager, followed closely by a top executive (including the CEO).[4] And while personally I found this desire for recognition from 'the big boss' slightly disconcerting, early in my career I was just as excited (and often terrified) to meet with my company's CEO or the CEO of one of my clients. Perhaps being close to — or even better, recognised by — the most senior people in an organisation reinforces a sense of an individual's importance, and gives them a sense of both meaning and belonging.

If you're a senior leader, don't underestimate the impact that you can have on engagement through your personal involvement in staff recognition. And even if you're not among the most senior leaders (yet!), remember that your personal recognition has an even greater impact on your direct reports than the CEO's!

In a healthy and engaged culture, recognition happens in all directions — not just top down. Peers recognise peers, junior people acknowledge guidance from experienced mentors, and teams recognise the contributions of other teams and external partners or suppliers.

In addition to talking frequently about the importance of building a recognition culture, there are a number of other techniques that I've seen work well to achieve this:

- peer recognition programs
- shared experiences
- reinforcing the value of gratitude.

Peer recognition programs

A low-cost peer recognition program can do wonders. Early in my career I was sent as a junior consultant to a bank in Texas. Talking to the CFO

---

[4] See gallup.com, 'Employee recognition: Low cost, high impact', by Annamarie Mann and Nate Dvorak.

one day, I noticed several gold cardboard stars sitting on the credenza behind his desk. 'What's with the stars?' I asked.

'Oh,' he said. 'That's our "Lone Star" recognition program. Each of us was given five of these stars,' he explained. 'And we were told that whenever someone does something good for you, you give them a star.'

A somewhat sheepish look briefly overtook the face of this tall, patrician Texan. 'You know, I thought it sounded pretty silly when they announced it. After all, I'm an accountant.' His face then brightened into a big smile. 'But you know, the first time someone handed me one of those stars, it felt pretty good!'

Years later, in my first big management job, I thought back to that Texan and his gold cardboard stars. We were trying to transform an outdated business model and one of the team had come up with the analogy of a frog called Freddy as the mascot for our business transformation.

We ordered several thousand 'frog' beanbags made up in multiple colours and placed them in 'ponds' (otherwise known as flower bowls) around the office. We explained to people that whenever someone did something good for them, they should grab a frog out of the nearest pond and give it to their colleague as a symbol of their recognition and thanks.

And it worked — boy, did it work. Frogs began appearing all over the office — proudly displayed on monitors and lined up on cubicle walls. 'Frog tossing' contests happened during lunch breaks. People painted and decorated their frogs. Frogs were arrayed in dioramas and comic poses. It was huge fun. It brought the whole business together as a team and gave us a clear identity: the formal recognition program became known as the Freddy awards. And most importantly — along with a number of other initiatives — it helped create a tremendous dynamic of transformation, interdependency and shared success that saw engagement scores skyrocket.

The total cost? Maybe $1500 across a thousand-person business. And a monthly email to all staff that said, simply, 'Frogs back in the pond', thereby restarting the process.

In recent years a number of digital models have emerged whereby staff send thanks to each other via e-greeting cards or digital vouchers.

I like the intent of these programs, and the fact that they make it easier to recognise people who are not physically adjacent. While some organisations swear by them, I personally haven't seen them lead to huge uptake among staff. In a world that's already overloaded with digital content, I suspect the engagement impact is inevitably less without some form of physical connection.

Peer recognition programs are a great way to:

- build a culture of appreciation around collaborative effort
- role-model behaviour
- reach out to customers or community.

The key is to get creative, keep it simple and make sure whatever you do aligns directly with the values and culture you're trying to reinforce.

Shared experiences

Another approach to building a broad-based recognition culture is through shared experiences that develop empathy and interdependence.

Many leadership development programs include some form of 360-degree feedback process, the results of which people are encouraged to share—in a confidential environment—along with their own personal history, working style and emotional challenges. Done well, this can bring a team together and create a sense of mutual support that naturally evolves into a recognition and celebration culture, since people understand better what's involved in each other's achievements.

A similar result can come through engaging in a difficult shared physical experience, where participants need to rely on each other to make it through.

Examples of this include walking the Kokoda Trail, competing in a corporate dragon boat event or completing a large group cycling tour. These challenges typically require extensive training before the main event, with participants recognising the need to support each other to push past previously known physical limits.

As there's a shared goal—the whole group needs to 'make it' to be successful—everyone gets practice at providing continuous encouragement and recognition, a habit that quickly translates back into the workplace. (As an added engagement benefit, shared adversity is known to help build strong friendships — which, in a work context, are also an important marker of high engagement.)

Reinforcing the value of gratitude

Reminding people of the value of gratitude is another way to encourage a recognition culture. There's a growing body of academic research that shows that gratitude is one of the key drivers of happiness — and that various interventions such as keeping a gratitude journal can make a big difference to the state of one's mental health.[5] If a critical mass of leaders in an organisation see the personal benefits of becoming deliberately grateful in their work and personal lives, this can quickly cascade into natural expressions of gratitude at work.

Informal AND formal

The discussion on gratitude highlights one of the most important subtleties of recognition programs: effective recognition doesn't always require money, certificates or promotions. Sometimes informal recognition — something as simple as a well-delivered thank you — can be even more effective.

In their book *The Power of Moments*, Chip and Dan Heath highlight the common elements of a great service experience — what they call an EPIC moment. According to the Heath brothers, memorable impact comes when an experience provides:

- *elevation:* an out-of-the-norm, 'peak' experience
- *pride:* recognition of an individual's specific contribution or achievement
- *insight:* an 'aha' moment of learning
- *connection:* deeper ties among or with members of the group.

---

[5] See, for example, health.harvard.edu, 'In praise of gratitude'.

The best forms of recognition follow a similar formula. Think back to the story at the beginning of this chapter:

- reading a compliment letter out loud, in front of several hundred of her peers, helped create an *unexpected, peak experience* for Jane

- the feedback was specific about what Jane herself had done, building *her pride* and *the pride of all* who worked with her

- the *surprising insight* that this letter came from a dying customer helped both Jane and the broader team recognise the value of her/their work

- the applause, the collective emotional experience and the hugs all helped Jane deepen her *connections* to the business and among the broader team.

You may not have the opportunity to celebrate such an extraordinary story on a regular basis. But based on the common mistakes I've seen, there are several guidelines for informal recognition that are worth highlighting:

- *Set expectations.* Be clear upfront that you will be giving people feedback, and make a point of highlighting when you're doing that, for example, 'Before we start this meeting, I just want to recognise what a great job Gary's doing on the merger plan.' Without highlighting the recognition, your good intentions can get lost in the fog of work.

- *Be specific.* Make sure people know exactly why they are being recognised. I've lost track of how many times I've asked a local 'employee of the month' why they won, only to be told they had 'no idea'.

- *Make it relevant.* Recognition should highlight outcomes or behaviours that are clearly aligned with the organisation's purpose and priorities. If you say that service is important, but always start a recognition discussion by celebrating the salespeople, your team will soon conclude what really matters to you.

- *Make it personal.* The nature of the actual reward should demonstrate a level of insight about what the individual really values. Maybe it's an individual's favourite biscuit at the end of a hard day; paying for a new mother's dinner out with her partner *and* a babysitter; or agreeing to a later start time during the season for an employee who coaches their daughter's swim practice. And remember that not everyone drinks wine or likes going to the football!

The exact manner in which recognition is delivered can vary widely — all it takes is a bit of creativity and the element of surprise (which, psychologically, embeds the positive recognition experience more deeply).

Whichever approach you choose, make sure that you are fully 'in the moment' when delivering recognition — for example, by applying the 'I see you' philosophy from chapter 1. Remember that the goal is to have a positive emotional impact, not to make the employee feel like they're part of an assembly-line process.

To stimulate your creativity, here are few examples of informal rewards that can make a big difference.

'Thank you' notes

While immediate messages and emails are welcome, the fact that digital communications are so pervasive makes the old-fashioned handwritten note even more impactful. As CEO I always kept a stock of personal notecards and envelopes on hand, and frequently dashed off notes to staff and customers to congratulate or thank them for a job well done.

One technique that can be immensely powerful is to write to an individual's family members — parents, partners and children. Shortly after graduating from college, my first boss wrote a letter to my father saying how well I was doing and how proud he should be of me. My father was over the moon — which had a bit to do with why I stayed there for a decade. Make them a hero in the eyes of their loved ones and they'll never forget it.

Birthdays, weddings, birth of a child, purchase of a new home, personal or family illness, Christmas cards, project milestones and career anniversaries are all opportunities to write personal notes that people will appreciate. But make sure it doesn't become an obvious 'factory': printed Christmas cards with a signature and no personal note go straight into my recycling bin (and do little for my sense of personal connection with the sender ...).

While I personally prefer the old-fashioned written note, I know that some companies use electronic thank-you-card systems to allow all employees to recognise and appreciate each other, with central tracking in place and copies sent to managers.

New opportunities

If you think creatively, there are lots of ways to both reward people and demonstrate care through new opportunities for growth and development. For example:

- *Exposure:* Ask the high performer to present at your next team meeting or town hall session on their work/project/insights/achievement. Or, invite them to shadow you or another senior colleague for a day.

- *Special projects or analysis:* Give people the chance to step out of their day-to-day roles and show what they can do. Help them build new relationships and gain visibility by presenting their findings to senior people whom they might not otherwise meet.

- *Conference attendance or study tours:* Give people the chance to meet industry peers and gain a bigger-picture perspective on your industry. If done in groups, these trips can also build personal relationships that enhance engagement.

- *Training courses:* Aside from internal and online courses, the chance to learn new skills and interact with others on an external course (such as, at a business school or industry association) can have a big impact on engagement. Similarly, paying for business school or providing a sabbatical to pursue study overseas can be a highly effective way of building loyalty and retaining high performers who are at a career crossroads.

- *Badges:* Following on from training, an increasing number of organisations are using the concept of 'badges' to recognise courses or accreditations earned by staff. These badges can be displayed physically or electronically, and in some cases are recognised across organisations. (This form of recognition is particularly helpful in roles where traditional career advancement options are not available.)

- *Coaching/mentoring sessions:* A one-on-one coaching session with the CEO or other senior leader, or mentoring by an external coach, can make a huge difference to the skills, confidence and emotional intelligence of a rising star.

- *Mentoring/team leadership:* Asking a high performer to mentor junior people or to lead a broader group are great ways to demonstrate respect and give them a chance to develop their own leadership skills.

- *Secondments and relief roles:* Giving people a chance to step up and act in another role — whether it's more senior or just in a different area — is a great way to build skills and pride. Just be careful to manage expectations about what happens when the secondment ends, so they don't end up demotivated when it's over!

- *Volunteering leave:* Many not-for-profits welcome the chance to host people who can bring their skills to bear. Offering to pay an employee's salary for a few weeks while they volunteer their time can be a great way to build their experience, personal satisfaction and loyalty.

Gifts

It really is the thought that counts. Demonstrate that you've put yourself in the shoes of the person you want to recognise, and the actual value becomes almost irrelevant. You might:

- buy doughnuts for a team that has been working through the night

- show up unannounced at a work site with boxes of pizza

- pay a celebrity on Cameo.com to record a pep talk for someone who's doing it tough
- buy a magazine subscription related to a colleague's hobby
- send a food hamper to a staff member who's just given birth
- take your whole team and their children to the opening of the latest Star Wars movie (dressed in costume, of course).

Some organisations have online gift catalogues and let their employees choose their own gift when they reach certain career milestones, or when their leaders want to recognise a particular achievement. While this might seem a little impersonal, it can still be effective when delivered as a pleasant surprise.

Commemorative gifts for completing big projects or deals can also have huge emotional impact. The Lucite 'tombstone' is the classic example in investment banking circles — although the ones that seem to get the most pride of place in offices are the mementoes that physically represent the project in some way — an engraved toy tractor for a farming transaction, for example.

One of the most emotionally impactful gifts I ever received at work was based on cryptic symbols I'd scribbled as a memory aid before an important external presentation: a team member noticed my notes and secretly had them engraved on some cufflinks, which they presented to me at a dinner after the event. And there's a reason why team t-shirts or fleece pullovers are so common: they build pride and connection, especially when they commemorate an achievement or common struggle.

If your company or industry has a long history, gifting an archival item — an old book, an antique piece of equipment, or even an old advertising poster — can help strengthen the ties between a high performer and the organisation. As a banker I collected antique money boxes on eBay, which I used as special gifts for valued staff and clients.

Just remember that with any gift, the key is to make sure it's delivered in a way that reflects the standards on recognition I described: make it personal, make it relevant and make sure people know why they're being recognised.

'Look at moi!'

Another fun way to recognise an individual's achievement is to give them a temporary privilege that makes them feel special. This could be the right to:

- wear a special shirt or badge
- sit at a special desk or chair
- be the proud owner of a special coffee mug
- display a particular award or sign
- choose the venue or menu for a team lunch
- represent their team at an external event.

Turn the tables

Asking high performers to do your job for a day, or to oversee you as you do *their* job for a day, is another way to make people feel special. As a leadership team, you can do this *en masse* by serving as bartenders or waitstaff at a private recognition event, cooking dinner for your team and their partners, or dressing up to entertain staff and their children at a family picnic.

While some of these ideas might sound a bit goofy — and obviously should reflect the culture and personality of the team — you'd be surprised how impactful they can be, even with relatively sophisticated people. Deep down, everyone wants to feel special!

I've deliberately left discussion of 'formal' recognition programs to later in the chapter, because too many leaders think recognition is all about formal programs and overlook all the informal ways in which they can build engagement.

Formal recognition — financial incentives, award programs, promotions and career advancement — obviously does have an important role in building and maintaining engagement. But there are a few subtleties to keep in mind if you want your investment in these programs to be effective.

Financial incentives

An entire industry is devoted to the design and assessment of financial compensation programs, and it's a topic that consumes immense attention and emotion from every stakeholder group.

While money clearly plays a *rational* role in attracting, retaining, incentivising and sometimes punishing behaviour, from an engagement standpoint it's more important to understand the *emotional* impact that you're trying to achieve.

'Wars are won by patriots, not mercenaries'

In a highly engaged organisation, financial incentives should be a secondary, rather than primary concern for staff. To put it bluntly, if the main reason that people work in your organisation is because of what they get paid, that's not engagement: it's bribery. And if you constantly focus on financial reward as the reason to feel good and work there, you are reinforcing to people that money is the basis on which they should feel engaged (or not).

You are also teaching them to evaluate other job offers on the basis of how much they pay — with the obvious risk to retention of high performers when times get tough. And you may inadvertently be sending them a message that financial performance is all that matters — to the detriment of service, compliance or ethical behaviour.

Even worse, you may create the perception — or reality — among the organisation's clients that your employees' interests are in conflict with doing the right thing for the client.

That doesn't mean money isn't important, or that people are being unreasonable if pay is an important consideration for them. No commercial organisation is going to maintain high engagement over time if its people feel they are being exploited through below-market pay.

However, it's worth bearing in mind that some 'financial' rewards have more perceived value than a straight salary increase (assuming, of course, that your people are already being paid fairly and competitively). For example, in markets such as the US that don't have universal health care, a generous health insurance plan takes on tremendous perceived value. Likewise:

- generous parenting leave policies
- extra vacation days
- long-service sabbaticals
- volunteering leave
- flex time or job-sharing arrangements

can all deliver to employees emotional value and engagement that transcend their salary.

In a highly engaged organisation, financial rewards are a marker of success, but not the objective. The message from leaders is: 'If you're doing well, you'll be paid competitively—and if we do well, you'll share in that success.'

When high performers asked me for a raise, I would often point out that any of our good people could always get an immediate pay rise by going somewhere else. But the question they *should* ask was, 'what happens after that?' In other words, they shouldn't assume that the change would lead to greater satisfaction, long-term career advancement, or superior pay. (They usually stayed.)

Compensation scheme design

This philosophy has a couple of implications for the design of compensation schemes.

First, it's important that bonuses or incentive payments—even for sales staff—retain an element of judgement by the leader. If they are too formulaic (that is, do *this* and get *that* dollar amount) then this reinforces a mercenary approach and undermines engagement.

As discussed in chapter 3, objective performance should factor into compensation decisions, but the eventual financial outcome should consider:

- behaviour relative to expectations
- the degree of difficulty and relative value of that individual's contribution

- any other adjustments for unanticipated upsides or downsides (for example, compliance breaches).

In the event of a disappointing outcome, this also helps the leader position the financial consequences in a way that doesn't make the individual feel personally de-valued.

Second, the amount of truly at-risk incentive[6] shouldn't be an excessive portion of a person's overall pay, unless the role is by definition an entrepreneurial one (such as a startup business executive) or the organisation itself is in the middle of a high-risk, high-return situation (such as a turnaround or high-risk merger transaction). Otherwise, the amount of money at risk can become mesmerising for the individual, regardless of the safeguards that are put in place.

Incidentally, the absolute amount of a financial reward doesn't have an enormous link to its emotional impact. A $250 gift certificate, if delivered in public with a heartfelt thank you for a specific job well done, can have a greater emotional impact than a $2500 quarterly bonus that arrives unheralded in one's pay cheque. It will certainly be remembered longer. What tends to matter more is the outcome *relative to expectations* — a fact that clever managers use with their team when approaching the annual pay cycle by talking down expectations.

Third, with very limited exceptions (for example, where dictated by union arrangements), adjustments to pay should happen on a regular review cycle rather than at random times based on job changes or people 'asking for a raise'. This is because frequent pay changes or reviews reinforce the idea that pay should be a central concern. I prefer to break the link between timing of promotions or job movements and what people get paid. So, for people whose contracts allow for variance in duties, an intra-year promotion would be followed up by a pay review on the regular schedule (which could potentially be back-dated to when they assumed the new role). This reinforces the idea that pay is not the main focus, but that it is reviewed competitively and systematically.

---

[6] Note that 'truly at-risk' indicates a distinction between true bonuses, which are paid based on stretching and uncertain outcomes, and 'variable pay' schemes, whereby a portion of one's pay is based on an expected target amount that can be varied up or down based on performance.

This *can* lead to tension in pay discussions from time to time, and there are times when you'll need to go the extra mile to keep a top performer. But my experience is that bowing to pressure on pay and giving in to the short-term sugar hit of an immediate pay rise doesn't tend to make the issue go away, or suddenly create a highly engaged staff member.

A steady and principled approach tends to work best to maintain engagement.

The other benefit of this approach is that it gives you the ability, on special occasions, to break your own rule and create an even greater recognition impact through an unexpected and unasked-for pay rise.

My final point is to think strategically about the structure of any financial incentives—how the size of reward is calculated, and how it's paid.

Cash amounts that are set in advance—such as, $5000 or $10 000 dollars—send a very 'transactional' signal, which can reinforce a mercenary perspective. By contrast, profit-sharing arrangements send a message of collective responsibility—'we're all in this together'.

Rounding off incentive amounts, rather than a formula calculated to two decimals, reinforces that the leader has made a judgement about the amount. In terms of structure, deferral arrangements or paying out in shares of stock (if a public company) are good ways to reinforce a psychological and emotional link to the organisation—thereby maximising the engagement value of the reward.

I have personally also seen great motivational value in using a small but fully discretionary pool for annual 'CEO awards'—typically a grant of $1000 to $10 000—that is allocated based on manager nominations of people who live the values or make extraordinary contributions beyond their role.

Award programs

Certificates, trophies, statuettes, names on plaques—the traditional manifestations of an awards program—still have remarkable value to people at all levels in organisations. They may seem old fashioned in a digital age, but I've never seen anyone display a printed-out e-certificate on their office wall (nor refer to it later online).

That's because the real value of these awards is not the award itself, but the memory it triggers and the achievement or recognition that it symbolises. So, if you want awards programs to have real engagement impact, you need to think carefully about the whole experience.

Special venues, dressing up, catering and special drinks, guest speakers, 'opening the envelope', acknowledgement speeches: all these things help to reinforce the recognition-value of awards and implant the memories deep in people's minds. Awards nights don't have to be overly expensive or fancy—but they do need to feel out of the norm.

While it may not always be feasible or economic, I'm a big fan of including the winner's partner or close friend in the celebrations—because it dials up the pride that people feel when they win. It also builds a further emotional connection if the people that are close to a staff member feel their own connection and empathy with the organisation.

Likewise, don't underestimate the power of ritual and symbols. If there is consistency to the way in which awards nights and similar celebrations take place, the impact on both the winners and the broader culture is stronger.

A ritual event becomes something that people look forward to, and talk about before and after the event, helping build connections. It provides a sense of order and predictability in their working lives.

With the right symbols—say, in the naming or design of the awards and ceremony—people find a deeper meaning in their achievements and a greater connection to the organisation and its history.

At my university, for example, it was traditional that no undergraduate could exit the campus through the main gate. Only after a traditional ceremony that included students in gowns and mortarboards, professors in multicoloured outfits, a call-and-response speech in Latin and presenting each student with an elaborate parchment diploma (also in Latin), did the whole class exit as one via that gate. Anachronistic? Probably. But it's no coincidence that the university's endowment is valued in the tens of billions of dollars—thanks to the generosity of its loyal alumni.

The same principle (minus the Latin) can be applied in a professional context as well.

CareerTrackers is an Australian not-for-profit started by Michael Combs. It helps young Indigenous students to get through university and find employment among major Australian companies. Each year an annual event recognises the participants who 'graduate' from the program by making it through university. In front of their families and friends, each student is called to the stage by the founder to receive their gift of a symbolic notebook, embossed with the CareerTrackers logo. Those who have graduated with honours from their university receive a special gold notebook.

While a notebook may not sound like an enormous gift, it immediately becomes one of the most prized possessions for these aspiring professionals, many of whom never expected to even go to university in the first place.

The *basis* on which awards are granted is also important.

The categories and selection criteria should reflect the overall values and priorities of the company. But it's also worth considering special awards that highlight the contributions of key culture-bearers in the organisation, as well as awards that are selected by the popular vote of peers rather than the leaders or HR organisation. Once again, positioning awards in this way can do a lot to make people feel valued and link recognition to the overall purpose and values of the organisation.

Individual AND team

While this discussion has focused primarily on individual awards and recognition, team recognition is also worth incorporating if your goal is to maximise engagement.

Many teams rely on 'quiet achievers' who may not have individually delivered something extraordinary but are nevertheless critical to the overall success of the team. Team awards allow those people to experience the same engagement benefits of appreciation and reward as individual achievers.

Aside from demonstrating that collective action is valued, team awards create stronger connections among team members and support a sense of friendly rivalry that can add to a sense of fun within the culture. Just make sure team competitions are held in a sense of fun, and that as the leader you reinforce that the real competition is outside the organisation, not inside.

Considering both individual and team recognition also serves to remind you to think about what sort of recognition best suits each individual. Leaders often forget that while some people love nothing more than to receive accolades on a stage, for others this is their biggest nightmare — to the point that they will actively avoid it. Recognising people in teams makes sure that these more self-effacing people get a positive benefit out of recognition, rather than a terrifyingly embarrassing experience.

Focused AND fair

Recognition programs need to be seen by employees as both focused and fair.

'Every child gets a prize' is not a recipe for reinforcing the benefits of hard work and commitment. You inevitably need to choose which aspects of performance or behaviour you are going to recognise — since one of the key engagement benefits of celebration is to reinforce what you want to see more of.

However, this raises three potential issues.

First, the things that you *don't* recognise may come to be seen as not important. So, when planning an awards program, think carefully about the range of categories you include and the symbolic messages you are sending in your choice of awards. In addition to sales or purely financial metrics, consider recognising achievements for:

- values and behaviour
- service quality
- project delivery
- people leadership
- teamwork
- cross-business collaboration.

Second, consider whether the selection criteria and process make it possible for '*any* child to get a prize'. In other words, if only certain roles within the organisation give people the opportunity to demonstrate outperformance, then there's a real danger that the broader organisation will see the recognition program as biased or unfair—thereby undermining the engagement value of the program.

For example, a sales recognition program based purely on total dollar value of sales may be biased to reward representatives in a wealthier territory where the average sale size is higher. Or, a leadership category that is judged purely by senior leaders may be seen to be biased in favour of staff who work in the head office.

To offset this risk, it's important to have an element of objective performance metrics as a screening mechanism in determining who gets rewarded. And, that there's a mechanism by which people in the field can nominate their team members or peers for awards in a way that overcomes any 'close-to-the-throne' bias.

It also follows that the selection process needs to be transparent, even if judgement is explicitly involved. Leaders need to get comfortable with saying, 'I/we considered a number of factors, and this is my judgement.'

Third, pay attention to the *relative* value of different awards—even if they aren't explicitly financial. People tend to have a strong focus on equity in rewards and assess their own level of satisfaction with how it sits relative to others. So, while it might be fine to reward one team with an overseas trip, and another one with a pub dinner, it's worth passing a 'fairness' lens over the whole program to identify any obvious inconsistencies that could create intramural resentment.

In the same way, be careful about the symbolism of how senior people are recognised and rewarded relative to more junior people. Over my career I've seen a number of senior executives undermine their credibility as leaders by being seen to lavish excessive perks—dinners, trips, gifts and so forth—on themselves and their own top teams. As small or seemingly justified as perks are, leadership shadows are long—and stories about corporate excess cast long leadership shadows.

Similarly, the choice of whom to recognise sends very clear signals to the organisation about what outcomes the leaders really value and what behaviour they really tolerate.

If you recognise people who live the values AND deliver good results, people will notice.

By contrast, recognising people who are seen to be ineffective, or whose behaviour is inconsistent with the stated values, will quickly undermine the value of your recognition programs.

Recognising leaders who achieve high engagement survey results is one way to reinforce the importance of the five points of the Leadership Star. But tread carefully: there is always a danger that bullying managers may demand that their team members submit high scores in order to make themselves look good.

At the same time, no organisation can maintain genuine engagement where it refuses to take action on leaders who consistently preside over low engagement scores. People rapidly become cynical if they perceive that leaders are promoting or protecting people based on favouritism or relationships with the leader rather than their demonstrated performance and values-driven behaviour.[7]

To avoid this risk, perform a formal 'performance and behaviour' screen to validate your decisions before finalising significant rewards and promotions. Review the individual's:

- recent performance outcomes
- staff engagement and retention scores
- 360-degree feedback results
- any compliance or behavioural complaints that may have been registered.

You might think that engineering a program to this extent risks undermining a high-performing, fast-moving, meritocratic culture, and there is a fine line to be drawn here. But if the objective of investing in a significant recognition program is to build and reinforce staff engagement, then it's important to be very deliberate in its design and execution.

---

[7] While this is inevitably subjective — people will always have different views on how their colleagues behave — behaviour can be quite different when the leader isn't watching, and leaders need to make an effort to identify those who 'manage up and kick down', or who deliver results without living the values.

CELEBRATE

Summary

Hopefully this chapter has broadened your perspective on both the importance of recognition and the many different ways in which it can be delivered to build engagement.

Organisations ask people to work hard, and let's face it—people have choices. Well-targeted recognition programs help bring meaning, emotional connection and pride to their efforts—all of which are critical to a highly engaged culture.

One final thought: make it fun! In this chapter we've looked at everything from thank-you notes to bean bag frogs, overseas trips and gala dinners. And while there's a place for formality and ritual, the opportunity to have fun and celebrate one's achievements with colleagues, family and friends can be even more important than a trophy or a few more dollars in the bank account.

So, don't be afraid to be creative, and even a bit silly, if it helps people come together to blow off steam and build stronger connections to each other and the organisation's mission. Just make sure that whatever you do, the people being recognised see the recognition as specific, relevant and personal.

Questions for reflection

- How often do you recognise your people's work, achievements and behaviour?

- How many different ways do you use to do this?

- Do you have a formal as well as informal recognition program? Does it include both financial and nonfinancial rewards?

- Do you explicitly use ceremony, tradition and ritual to build emotional connections among people and to the organisation?

- Do the categories of recognition align to the organisation's priorities and values?

- Do people see it as transparent, fair and equitable?

- Thinking about the individuals you most recently recognised, what implicit messages did you send to your people about what was important to you?

- Are all forms of recognition sufficiently specific, relevant and personal?

PART II
Growing as a Leader

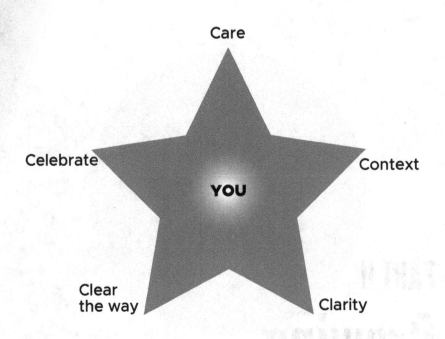

6

YOU

'I did it!'

Angela beamed as she walked into my office.

'The first campaign is out the door!' If it's possible to smile with your whole body, Angela was doing it. She was literally bouncing with enthusiasm.

'That's fantastic,' I said. 'What happened?'

'Well, I managed to convince John Rock to re-prioritise the statement run and to let our operations team have access to the system so we can open the new accounts.'

'Well done! See, I *told you* you could do it,' I said with a mischievous grin.

'Yeah, yeah, I know. Anyway, thanks! I'm taking the team to lunch now ... see you later!' Angela bounced out of the office, leaving behind the infectious glow of her joy.

For the past several months Angela had been in a very different state. Her initial enthusiasm for the role had devolved into frustration and emotional volatility. It seemed that nearly every week she was in my office in tears, angry and frustrated at yet another roadblock that had been thrown in her way, or an obstinate manager who had refused to help.

Angela's 'campaign manager' role was a new one, designed to work across the organisation to coordinate direct sales of products to customers, without requiring them to go into a bank branch (this was the mid 1990s, and most sales still required a physical meeting to complete). That meant we — and Angela in particular — were essentially making it up as we went, designing new processes and adapting old technology to a new approach.

This wasn't the way the organisation was wired to work, and a number of old-timers weren't interested in changing things — hence the roadblocks.

As Angela's direct manager, I found our weekly meetings pushed me into the role of consultant, psychiatrist and cheerleader. This was uncomfortable territory for me — I hadn't had any formal leadership training, and my previous management experience was in overseeing teams of junior consultants. These were mostly self-motivated over-achievers: the only real 'management' required was to point them towards their latest assignment.

Deep down, I still saw myself as one of them — someone whose satisfaction came from my own individual achievements and recognition.

But when Angela and her smile walked out of my office that day, the wave of satisfaction that hit me was almost physical. I felt an extraordinary pride in having helped Angela to be successful — like Dr Seuss's Grinch, my heart grew three sizes that day.

The next day, I still felt it. The following week, I was still smiling about what she'd achieved. And more than 20 years later, I still smile as I remember where she was standing, where I was standing, and how it made me feel as I watched her beam with pride in her achievement.

The conversation with Angela was brief, but it was one of the most momentous in my professional career. Because it taught me that I got far more satisfaction from helping *other* people succeed than I did from my own successes.

Every star has its source of energy, and power. For the Leadership Star, that source is *you*.

As leadership scholar Warren Bennis said, 'Becoming a leader is synonymous with becoming yourself. It's precisely that simple, and it's also that difficult.'

You can go through the motions on Care, Context, Clarity, Clear the way and Celebrate, and it will improve engagement — for a while, at least.

But if you aren't genuinely committed to the organisation's purpose, and authentic in the way you engage with people, they will see through it. And they will wonder why they should commit themselves, or give any extra effort, when their leader clearly isn't committed to walking the talk themselves.

Think about the top ten most valuable brands in the world as of 2020.[1]

1. Amazon

2. Google

3. Apple

4. Microsoft

5. Samsung

6. ICBC

7. Facebook

8. Walmart

9. Ping An

10. Huawei.

Then think about some of the other highly respected companies that didn't quite make the list: Disney, Tesla, IBM, Nike, Virgin. With a few exceptions, I bet you can name the famous founders of these companies.[2]

Coincidence? No. These founders brought so much energy and passion for their business and their corporation's values that they became the embodiment of their organisation. And among their people, this built loyalty and commitment that extended to people who'd never met

---

[1] See visualcapitalist.com, 'Ranking the world's most valuable brands', January 2020.

[2] Jeff Bezos (Amazon), Larry Page & Sergey Brin (Google), Steve Jobs (Apple), Bill Gates (Microsoft), Lee Byung-chul (Samsung), Mark Zuckerberg (Facebook), Sam Walton (Walmart), Ma Mingzhe (Ping An), Ren Zhengfei (Huawei), Walt Disney (Disney), Elon Musk (Tesla), Tom Watson (IBM), Phil Knight (Nike), Richard Branson (Virgin).

the founder, and in some cases has outlasted the life of the founder themselves.

It's often said in HR circles that 'people don't leave companies, they leave managers'. So, if you're seeing significant voluntary turnover in a team — or among your own direct reports — then the source of the issue probably sits with the leader, not the team.

The alternative is also true — for people to truly buy into an organisation's mission, they need to buy into their leaders as well.

If you want to build engagement that lasts, you need to be prepared to work on yourself as much as on your people — to be part teacher and part student. You need to stay humble and keep looking to improve in ways that help your people be better. This is as true when you're starting out as a leader as when you're already the CEO.

If you've come to this book because you're concerned about the low level of engagement in your team, there's a reasonable chance that this issue is as much about *you* as it is about *them*. And remember that highly effective people leaders don't start off as the complete package — they continue to work on themselves.

In particular, there are four areas where successful, highly engaging leaders stand out:

1. personal values and purpose
2. self-awareness
3. empathy
4. energy.

Each of these is a large topic in itself, and full coverage of them is beyond the scope of this book. But here are a few key lessons I've learned over time that you may find helpful.

1. Personal values and purpose

Chapter 2 focuses on the importance of getting clear on the organisation's mission or purpose. As an individual leader, you need to get clear about your own purpose.

If you can't clearly articulate in your own words what you're about and what really matters to you, then it is worth finding the time and headspace to do so:

- Why do you do what you do?
- What contribution do you want to make in your career, and in this role?
- What principles do you want to live your life by?
- What change do you believe is needed in your industry?
- How does working in this role at this organisation serve these goals?

The more you can get clear on the answers to questions like these, the more authentic your leadership will be.

You may feel that you're already clear on this — perhaps your current job or industry felt like a calling from the beginning. However, the constant treadmill of work and personal commitments, and the energy required to meet monthly or quarterly targets, can often get in the way of deep reflection on issues such as purpose and values.

Think about the important choices you've made in your life and the way you've responded to significant challenges and opportunities. As the old saying goes, actions speak louder than words. You may have self-talk or a stated set of goals that you fall back on, but your actions in times of stress are a bigger clue to what's really important to you.

Similarly, think about the personal values that define your character — for example, integrity, courage, care for others, dependability and grit. Now consider: have you earned your colleagues' trust by always acting in ways that are consistent with these values?

Talking these issues through with a coach, mentor or trusted friend is a good way to get the ideas out of your head. Or, consider actually writing out your answers to a few key questions, in a document that only you will read. Before becoming CEO of Westpac, I prepared a 'Personal Leadership Statement', using an approach outlined by Terry Pearce in his excellent book, *Leading Out Loud*. The questions outlined in the book were enormously helpful to me in clarifying my own purpose and motivations, and over the course of the next few years I often referred back to this document to help re-centre myself when things got tough.

While part of this self-examination is to set aspirations that go beyond today's reality, the most important thing is to be honest with yourself about what's *really* true and important to you.

Once you're clear on your *personal* motivations, make sure you think carefully about how they line up with the leadership role you're performing and the mission and values of the organisation. You made a choice to take this role, and to be a leader in this organisation—make sure you can explain *why* to your team members. If your people don't understand your thinking, they will make assumptions and fill in the gaps for themselves, and not necessarily in a positive way.

Ultimately, you need to be able to say to your people, with conviction: 'Here's what I'm about; here's what I stand for; here's why I've chosen to be here; here's what I believe we need to do as a team to fulfil the organisation's mission; and here's why I believe in our ability as a team to achieve it.'

Once you believe and can articulate this to your team, your authenticity and commitment will do wonders for your team members' personal commitment, confidence, and loyalty to both you and the organisation.

2. Self-awareness

A top executive recruiter once told me that the single most important determinant of executive success is self-awareness.

Why? From what I've observed, people with low self-awareness often fail to recognise their own potential career 'derailers' and are thus more likely to make terminal mistakes.

Meanwhile, people with *high* self-awareness:

- know what their strengths are, and use them to their advantage
- know what their weaknesses are, and work to improve or neutralise them

- are more able to connect with others and maintain relationships

- understand their underlying fears and vulnerabilities, and are better able to manage them through periods of stress or conflict.

High self-awareness allows you to demonstrate congruity between your stated purpose, the organisation's purpose and what it is that you're asking people to do. Without it, people can misinterpret your commitment to the organisation and thus question their own.

As human beings we tend to judge ourselves by our intentions, and to judge others by their behaviour. Understanding how your behaviour is perceived by others is therefore critical to making sure that the impact you have on your team is consistent with your intentions.

As you get more senior in an organisation, self-awareness tends to reduce rather than increase. This is because there are fewer senior people willing to give you unvarnished feedback, and more junior people trying to curry favour by telling you only positive things.

It's worth noting that there are two types of self-awareness for leaders to work on:[3]

1. *internal self-awareness:* how well we understand our own internal motivations, aspirations, strengths and weaknesses, and emotional drivers

2. *external self-awareness:* how well we understand how others see us, how they assess our motivations and how they are likely to react to our actions.

Internal self-awareness

Getting clear on your own personal values and purpose — as already discussed — is an important way to build internal self-awareness.

It can also help to work with a coach or psychologist to understand how your own experience and emotions shape your reactions to situations.

---

[3] For a more complete explanation, see 'What self-awareness really is (and how to cultivate it)', by Tasha Eurich, *Harvard Business Review*, January 2018.

I know from personal experience that getting to the bottom of your emotional 'scars' can be a confronting and painful process. But the payoff is worth it.

With the assistance of my coach, I came to understand that a number of aspects of my childhood — my parents' divorce, my relationship with my father and the breakdown of an important friendship — were having a significant ongoing effect on how I interacted with people at work. My insecurities about relationships and desire to be liked were getting in the way of having difficult conversations with colleagues and making it harder for me to stand up to bullies or people in positions of power when I had genuine disagreements.

As an ex-consultant, insecurities about my own management skills meant that I kept trying to justify my role by being the 'smartest guy in the room', rather than trusting my team members and spending more time listening than talking.

By working with a coach, I learned to be able to remain calm in times of crisis and to keep my ego in check despite the glare of public scrutiny. And importantly, I became more adept at managing my emotions in times of stress.

Emotional unpredictability and volatility — especially personal anger, disdain or anything that looks like bullying behaviour — is an enormous negative for sustaining engagement. These outbursts happen when an individual or a specific situation pushes one of the leader's historical 'hot buttons', thereby triggering an emotional response.

Gee, that's interesting

One approach that has helped me maintain a 'cool and calm' demeanour over the years is to have a 'Gee, that's interesting' conversation with myself when under stress.

This technique is as follows:

1. Notice you are having a stress or anxious reaction (for example, higher pulse rate, butterflies in the stomach, rising nervousness or anxiety).

2. Say to yourself, 'Gee, that's interesting — I notice that I'm feeling stressed/anxious. I wonder why that is?'

3. Consider what it is about this particular situation that is bringing up an emotional response. (Usually, it reminds you of a bad past experience or personal insecurity.)

4. Once identified, say to yourself, 'Oh yes — it's *X* again.' (I find the mere identification of the cause is usually enough to blunt the anxiety.)

5. Consider what other reaction or steps may be needed in the situation and make a positive choice how to respond.

Over time you'll get clearer on the list of things that push your buttons and will be much more able to maintain your equanimity.

Passion and energy are important traits in a leader — I'm not suggesting you need to become dull. But being able to control your negative emotions creates a calmer, more predictable environment that will help your people feel settled and engaged.

External self-awareness

External self-awareness — knowing how others see and react to you — is equally important.

As human beings, we tend to be pretty bad at understanding *why* someone else does what they do. And worse, we often assume that others have bad intent.[4] The danger is that a leader who is doing something that they believe to be 'for the good of the firm' can be seen by their people to be acting out of selfishness, favouritism, personal ambition or spite.

So how do you build *external* self-awareness?

One of the most common tools is 360-degree feedback. This relies on surveys of an individual's manager, direct reports and peers to gain feedback on their behaviour and effectiveness, which is then shared with the individual directly (sometimes with anonymous comments).

While you need to be careful not to read too much into these reports ('it's only feedback — that doesn't make it true', as one of my former bosses used to say), these surveys can highlight issues or perceptions that

---

[4] See *Thinking, Fast and Slow* by Daniel Kahneman for a discussion of this and other cognitive biases.

you might otherwise not hear from people directly. In my first 360-degree report, I was confronted with a particular issue (about collaboration) that I felt was unfair. It was only after several months of grumbling and denigrating the report that I came to realise that there was an important truth in the feedback, which led me to substantially change how I interacted with my peers.

Another good technique for building self-awareness is to seek written feedback directly. For example, whenever I start a new job I ask people in the business to write me a letter that answers five key questions:

1. What do we need to keep?

2. What do we need to change?

3. What do you most hope that I will do?

4. What do you most fear that I will do?

5. Do you have any other advice for me?[5]

Not only did the responses give me insight about what needed to be changed, they also revealed people's expectations for me and the broader leadership team. This was helpful in understanding how to position the changes that we ultimately made in ways that helped rather than hurt engagement (that is, by linking changes back to staff feedback).

In one-on-one meetings, people are often nervous about giving negative feedback to their boss. But if 'have you got any feedback for me?' is a standing agenda item over time, it demonstrates your genuine willingness to hear and learn from your people. Consider asking this question at the beginning of the meeting, rather than the end, so that you don't run out of time and it doesn't seem like a throw-away question that you don't really want answered.

It's worth remembering that even the most senior executives still want to be liked and may not feel comfortable giving direct negative feedback. Asking your boss 'have you got any feedback for me?' might therefore

---

[5] A similar approach is to require everyone to complete two lists highlighting areas to 'Start, Stop, Do More and Do Less'. One list is for the business, and one for the culture. By sharing the results of this survey with staff immediately, one CEO figures he builds a year's worth of trust nearly instantly, by being transparent and addressing which issues he will tackle, and which he won't (and why).

be too confrontational for them to answer honestly. If this is the case, a better strategy is to de-personalise the issue by asking: 'Is there anything you've seen me do, or not do, that you think I could have handled better?' This makes the conversation about the *behaviour*, rather than about *you*, and is more likely to elicit an insight or feedback that helps you avoid problems down the road.

To have a broader impact in the organisation, it's important to role-model your desire for feedback and willingness to confront the difficult issues. For example, consider sharing your 360-degree feedback report with your team and asking for comments and clarifications. Make sure to thank people for being so open, especially if aspects of the feedback are confronting. You may feel that some of the feedback is unfair but do not argue the point: how you respond will affect their willingness to be open in the future. Tell them what you're going to do about the feedback, and ask them to hold you to account.

One CEO I know solicits feedback on his performance from staff across the organisation, and then shares it in town hall meetings. After sharing a particularly tough piece of feedback, he might say, 'I'm devastated by that, and thank you for sharing it. Here's what I'm going to do ....' The courage required for these sorts of conversations sets a great example for other leaders in the organisation.

A final suggestion about building self-awareness is to make it a game. Before you go into a meeting with someone or a group of people, make a prediction to yourself about how they will react to you and what you have to say. What body language do you expect? Do you expect them to agree with you? To be positive, or to be difficult?

If the reaction you get is different than what you expected, this could be a good sign that you need to work on your external self-awareness. Find someone you can trust — a colleague, a boss or an external coach — and ask them to help.

3. Empathy

When I reflect on the leaders I've known who consistently build highly engaged teams, one personality trait stands out: empathy.

Remember Miriam from chapter 1, who had sky-high engagement from her team, despite them all being fired?

One thing I *didn't* tell you about that story is that Miriam is not the typical Anglo-Australian female executive. Aside from being incredibly energetic, positive and disciplined, she is a practising Muslim of South-Asian descent who wears a headscarf to work. For years, I had assumed that this would have made her task even harder, given that she was going into a business that was predominantly comprised of Hong Kong Chinese people.

In fact, Miriam says her background made her task much *easier*: 'They could see that that I understood cultural context in making and communicating our decisions,' she told me.

For example, Miriam went on, 'Our building had a meditation room, and the entire team would go there on a regular basis to meditate. It gave everyone a safe place to be angry and upset, but also to bring balance to those emotions.'

That empathy extended beyond Miriam herself to her broader leadership team: 'In Asian culture, "face" is important, and losing your job can bring a great loss of face to a family. Without me knowing it, some of our most experienced people went home with our younger staff members to meet their parents and explain that although their child was losing their job, they had done nothing wrong.'

Is it any surprise that, nearly 20 years on, Miriam is still in touch with many of her team members, who still consider themselves a family?

As discussed in chapter 1, the best leaders genuinely care about their people and continuously take steps to demonstrate that fact.

Some seem to have a sixth sense for working out how people are feeling and what's concerning them, and playing that understanding back in a way that builds trust. They show that beyond an intellectual understanding of people, they actually *share* in what they are feeling.

Although some people seem to be born empathisers, certain aspects of leadership can play against the development of empathy. The more senior you become, the more removed from the day-to-day activities of your people you may be. Likewise, as people move up the ladder in an organisation, they may find themselves responsible for people from different walks of life who perform roles that they themselves have never done. And there's also the phenomenon, discussed in the last section, of people not wanting to complain or give bad news to more senior people — thereby allowing the false conclusion that things are okay.

The challenge for leaders is to stay curious, open-minded and willing to feel uncomfortable. Ask open-ended questions, while resisting the temptation to be in 'telling mode' all the time. Spend time with parts of the organisation that you don't normally deal with, walking in their shoes whenever possible. Meet with people in their environment, rather than yours, so that they are more likely to open up. And don't be afraid to ask dumb questions about things you 'should know already', and to try your hand on the tools.

Company picnics, offsites and town hall meetings are also an opportunity to humanise the leaders. Depending on the culture, a willingness to dress in silly outfits, be the target of a 'dunking' machine, or endure a good-natured ribbing from your direct reports can go a long way to showing that you are approachable and don't take yourself too seriously.

It's also important to know and manage your own biases. We've all got them: age, gender, culture, race, language or accents, sexual preferences, geography, educational or career backgrounds can all lead to positive and negative biases. These biases can lead us to miss important insights, make poor judgements about people, or make some people feel unwelcome or disaffected.

Too many leaders think they need to maintain a distance from their people in order to preserve their authority. When it comes to engagement, I believe the opposite is true.

Leaders need their people to trust them if they're going to become engaged. And an important contributor to trust is *vulnerability*. This is because a willingness to be vulnerable demonstrates:

- a level of underlying self-confidence

- a commitment to transparency

- a willingness to let others be vulnerable too.

One good way to demonstrate vulnerability is to publicly 'step up', apologise and take accountability when things go wrong. Aside from earning people's respect, this sets a good standard for other leaders in the organisation.

The more your people respect you as a person, and believe you understand how they feel, the more they will put their heart into working for you and the organisation.

Look for symbolic ways to show that you 'get' them and their job, and that you honour and respect them for it. Walk the floor at random, and don't just talk to the senior people. Show up unexpected at events and celebrations that are important to them. Donate to their causes. Listen humbly to complaints. Attend funerals. Wear green on St Patrick's Day, if that's a thing at your workplace. And don't EVER use your seniority to cut the queue in the local café. (PS: Getting to know the staff at the local café is a great way to find out how people are *really* feeling!)

4. Energy

Leadership can be tiring. If you are genuinely committed to serving your people, the physical and emotional toll over time is large.

Highly engaged teams need to see that their leaders are human, but they also need to see that their leaders are positive and committed to doing what's needed to achieve the organisation's mission and goals.

For the leader, this means managing your energy well so you can demonstrate a consistent level of enthusiasm and commitment to your team. The more senior you are, the more this is true: CEOs can't afford off days.

Lots of sleep, exercise, nutrition, and giving yourself mental and emotional space are all important. It's a cliché, but leadership is a marathon, not a sprint.

I am by no means Superman when it comes to physical self-discipline — I drank far too much coffee and ate way too much chocolate during my time as CEO. But over the course of my career I did learn a few things that may be helpful in sustaining your own leadership energy:

- *Prioritise sleep.* Leaders need to stay emotionally balanced and able to think clearly in a crisis. You can't do that if you're exhausted. Being well rested makes it much easier to think clearly about both the current situation and the future. When you're tired, all you do is react.

- *Learn to switch off.* For some people it's exercise, while for others it's time with family, food and wine, music, movies, binge TV, travel or even video games. Whatever helps you switch off, do it — and don't feel guilty. Your subconscious brain needs time to process everything that you're dealing with. (I find cycling, dinners with my family, reading and the odd video game help me switch off.)

- *Find your source of energy at work.* I found that time spent with customers and front-line people brought me great joy and energy. I also have a passion for digital technology, the use of data in marketing and great advertising. There will inevitably be aspects of your job that you love, and parts that you don't. As you become more senior, it's important to allow yourself to indulge your passions at least occasionally.

- *Laugh, a lot.* While business is serious, and the obligations of leadership are many, it's important not to take yourself too seriously. In my experience the most engaged teams are both focused and relaxed with each other in ways that lead to lots of laughter. Obviously, there's a time and a place to be serious — but to me a sign of a great team is one that can go from a brutally frank confrontation about a business issue to laughter in the space of a few minutes.

YOU

Summary

Highly engaging leaders are *authentic*. They know who they are, and what they stand for. They're not perfect—no-one is. But they work hard to understand where they are strong, and where they are weak. They encourage feedback, even when it's painful, because they know that it will make them better. Their actions and behaviour are aligned with their words and intentions.

This is not about trying to be some idealised leader, or to be someone that you're not. Quite the contrary—it's about facing reality and demonstrating a commitment to trying to get better that your people can respect.

Most of all it's about recognising that the opportunity to lead other people—to help them achieve and to become better than they thought they could ever be—is an amazing, honourable and fulfilling gift that is much more satisfying than any recognition for your individual success.

Questions for reflection

- What do you stand for as a person? What are your personal values?

- Why do you choose to work here?

- How do you see yourself serving your team and your organisation?

- What difference do you want to make?

- Why is that important to you?

- What issues in the past are holding you back in your relationships with colleagues?

- What would you do if you weren't afraid?

- When is the last time you had a 360-degree feedback assessment done?

- What did you learn, and what did you do about it?

- Do you have a coach or mentor that you trust completely? If not, who can you go to for some straight feedback and wise counsel?

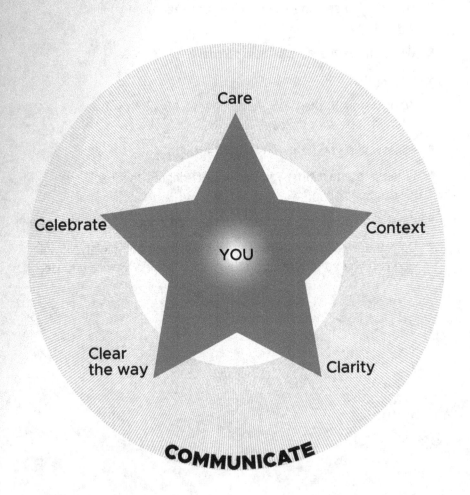

COMMUNICATE

Have you ever been to Disney World?

Several years ago, I took my whole family — wife, six kids and mother-in-law — from Australia to Orlando, Florida, for a once-in-a-lifetime holiday. We had a great time, and it's still one of my family's favourite holidays.

From start to finish — from planning the trip online to the photos and offers we received when we got home — the service experience was incredible. Before leaving, we planned the trip in an online calendar and received personalised bag tags in the post. That meant that after checking our bags in at Sydney airport we didn't touch them again until they arrived in our hotel room. 'Magic wristbands' meant we didn't have to fumble for tickets or payment cards at any point. A mobile app helped us navigate to rides with short queues and book a table in a nearby restaurant. And expert photographers took family photos and uploaded them to a private website for us to view back in the room. Disney had thought of everything.

Little did I know that the trip would turn out to be one of the most important trips in my business life too.

While I was there, I was introduced by a colleague to Tom Boyles, a senior executive with Disney Resorts who oversaw their investment in data and digital platforms that underpinned much of the innovation I was experiencing. Tom explained to me that the whole point was to eliminate hassles for each member of the family *so that we would come back.*

I realised that there were enormous parallels for banking — in essence, we too were a service business, not a product business, and we needed to think creatively about how the combination of people and technology could create an experience that would get people and their families to bank with us forever.

When I got back, I told the story of our trip — including the experience and the insights that Tom Boyles had shared — to a group of high-potential staff, challenging them to imagine our future much as Disney had imagined theirs. Excited and engaged by the Disney example, they came up with a series of new service offerings and product designs that formed the basis of a whole new strategy for the bank — what I came to call 'The Service Revolution'.[1]

More broadly, by telling the story of my trip and the innovations it had inspired, I was able to excite and motivate thousands of staff to adopt our new service-focused business strategy. And more than seven years later, people still remind me of 'the Disney story' and how important service has become to them as a core value of the company.

As a piece of communication, that one story played an immense part in helping build engagement during my time at Westpac. It cut through all of the other messages emanating from senior management and helped each employee connect at a personal level with the corporation's strategy: who doesn't want to go to Disney World?!

Communication — focused, effective and ongoing — is critical to building and sustaining staff engagement. It's so important I considered calling Communication the sixth point of the Leadership Star. But since you can't implement any of the five points of the star *without* communication, and since remembering more than five things in a list is nearly impossible, I settled for a separate chapter with tips on how communications can help you build engagement.

You've probably heard sayings such as 'tell them what you're going to tell them, tell them, then tell them what you've told them'. And if

---

[1] Tom Boyles was excited by this too: 18 months later he joined my team at Westpac to help lead the transformation.

you've ever repeated a shopping list in your head over and over again to remember it, then you know that our brains need to hear things multiple times in order to remember them.

In a working environment, the problem of remembering messages is exacerbated by the twin challenges of distraction and change.

Most people are so busy dealing with their inbox and current priorities that they don't have time to focus on big-picture issues such as mission, vision and values. And even if they walk out of a big presentation feeling excited, the reality of deadlines and a growing inbox can quickly bring them back to earth.

Plus, if someone has been working at an organisation for a reasonable period of time, it's not uncommon for 'change fatigue' to set in. This might be a function of changes in business priorities, in messaging, or changes in the senior management themselves — each coming in excited to share their own new messaging and priorities. If people have had three senior managers in the last two years, is it any wonder that they're a bit cynical about the new mission statement?

The only way to overcome this challenge (aside from clearing out people who absolutely refuse to get on board) is clear and consistent communications. And this requires far more than a few presentations and the occasional email to staff.

There are four main lessons I've learned about using communications to drive engagement:

1. build a structured communications plan

2. use multiple channels to target your audience

3. design messages that stick

4. listen, adjust and keep at it.

1. Build a structured communications plan

Each of the five points of the Leadership Star — Care, Context, Clarity, Clear the way and Celebrate — requires both initial and ongoing communication. Depending on the size of your team and the overall organisation, this can imply a large number of messages that need to be delivered to different groups of people over a period of time.

If you're committed to building engagement using the Leadership Star, you simply can't wing it. But happily, this planning exercise doesn't have to be too time-consuming or complicated.

A simple approach that has worked well for me over the years is to lay out a spreadsheet with columns for each month of the year and rows for each major stakeholder group that you want to engage: direct reports, managers, front-line workers, peers, board/senior management, and so on. (You might also decide to include some key customers or business partners in this stakeholder list if you want to combine this with any other non-engagement-related planning you're doing.)

In each cell of that matrix you identify the key engagement goal(s) for that month and the method you'll use to get that message out.

For example, you might decide on a quarterly town hall meeting with all the people managers in your area, followed by a five-minute video interview to be sent out to all staff a few days later.

Once you've laid this out for the year, go back and check that you'll be covering each of the five points of the Leadership Star for each of the stakeholder groups. You can then diarise the planning and execution of each of these communications into your calendar.

As CEO I met quarterly with my communications team to update the plan and work through the contents of upcoming communications. This allowed us to:

- review recent staff surveys or feedback on engagement issues
- consider the impact of external events on our people
- adjust our internal messaging and priorities accordingly.

You don't need your own communications team to plan and deliver an effective engagement program. You just need to take the time to think through the various stakeholder groups you want to reach, and how often, and make these activities a priority by building them into your schedule in advance.

2. Use multiple channels to target your audience

Chances are that your organisation already uses a variety of communication mechanisms to take the pulse and build engagement. But in the same way you can't rely solely on a formal approach to recognition, it's important not to be too reliant on formal communication channels such as quarterly 'all-in' briefings and a monthly email.

If you've worked through your communications plan carefully, you'll no doubt have realised that there are different segments of your team, each with different perspectives that shape how they view any communications.

For example, front office sales and service people tend to view things through the eyes of the customers they deal with every day. Technologists may form their perspectives based on the size and effectiveness of investments in upgrading the organisation's technology stack. Finance staff tend to think about how an organisation's plans are likely to affect the bottom line. And people who have been with the organisation for years may simply feel that they've heard it all before.

This means that you can't rely on broadcasting a small number of mass communications — such as, conference speeches, video messages or email newsletters — to connect and engage everyone in an organisation. A base level of consistent messaging is good, but true engagement requires a level of narrowcasting as well.

Similarly, don't rely purely on internal communication channels to get your message out: employees are often highly aware of how their organisation is portrayed externally, so remember that external messages (advertising, media interviews, speeches and the like) can be highly effective at targeting internal audiences.

While a well-designed communication of the organisation's purpose and priorities will likely resonate regardless of an individual's specific role, recognising that different people have different lenses can help you think about how to shape and target your message in a way that different groups of people can understand and connect with it.

Appendix B provides a detailed discussion on each of the various communication channels you might want to use, their role in building engagement, and a few do's and don'ts.

Table 7.1 is a summary, along with some of the key success factors that I've picked up over time.

Table 7.1: Communication channels

Channel	Best for ...	Key success factors
Large group presentations and conferences	• Direct to masses • Sense of occasion and cut-through • Creating a shared experience	• Prepare and rehearse • Avoid death by PowerPoint • Involve the audience • Celebrate the locals • Have a 'wow factor'
Communication workshops and cascade meetings	• Launching company-wide initiatives • Ensuring consistent messages • Creating buy-in and culture change	• Top team is engaged • Messages and stories are agreed on • Sessions are leader-led • Include facilitator packs • Everyone is included
Smaller town hall meetings	• Team engagement • Humanising leaders • Showcasing talent • Two-way dialogue • Getting feedback	• Minimal slides • Limited scripting • Small panels (2–3 people) • Authenticity • Informal Q&A
Team visits, floor-walks	• Unfiltered learning • Demonstrating care • Understanding real life for employees	• Keep it unscripted • Minimal 'handling' by senior people • Prepare: learn names, roles, issues, questions • Visit back of house
Business and project reviews	• Learn business detail • Accelerate progress • Build engagement • Spot and grow talent	• Use Session D format (page 89) • Have clear presentation guidelines • Encourage junior contributions • Avoid public criticism that undermines confidence

Channel	Best for ...	Key success factors
Skip-level meetings	• Get to know team • Understand team priorities/issues • Directly communicate priorities • Get feedback on direct reports	• Make them open-ended, with a limited agenda • Encourage participation by all • Observe team dynamics • Request constructive feedback on team's leader
Informal coffees/lunches	• Take soundings across organisation • Identify hidden issues and barriers • Build network of advocates	• Make them open-ended, with a limited agenda • Minimise intimidation (casual venue, catering, and so on.) • Send follow-up thank you
One-on-one communications	• Celebrate milestones • Demonstrate care • Express thanks	• Schedule time to do them • Keep it brief • Personalise the messages • Include surprise factor
Email, blogs, webchats, internal social media	• Mass communications • Reinforce through consistency • Humanise leaders • Get unvarnished feedback	• Make sure it sounds like you • Put key message in first paragraph • Avoid buzzwords • Encourage and respond to direct feedback
'Wallpaper' (that is, visual clues via posters, door surrounds, coffee cups, and so on.)	• Reinforce high-level messages in physical environment • Remind people of expectations • Build pride	• Avoid excess 'sloganeering' • Use real staff in pictures • Rotate to keep it fresh • Use occasional surprises
External communications and social media	• Build pride • Reinforce staff messages on purpose, values and priorities • Set customer and business partner expectations	• Recognise staff impact of external messages • Use social media to engage staff and industry participants • Use customer advertising to reinforce values, purpose and priorities to staff

As you can see, there are a multitude of different ways to get your message out — and successful leaders use them all to reinforce the messages that build engagement.

Good communications depend on having good messages — so let's turn now to the *content* side of communication design.

3. Design messages that stick

I framed the Leadership Star as five 'Cs' so that the steps required to build engagement were easy to remember, without referring back to this book. And if I've done a *really* good job, thinking of the Cs will quickly prompt you to recall key stories like those of Miriam in Hong Kong, the bricklayer and the cathedral, and the broken copy machine — helping you to consider whether you're doing everything you can to build engagement.

In the same way, the engagement messages you deliver — regardless of the channel — need to be easily recalled by your employees — or all that effort goes to waste.

In other words, you need to design messages that stick.

But how?

Make it a SUCCES

In their hugely enjoyable and insightful book *Made to Stick*, Dan and Chip Heath crack the code on why some communications stick with their audience, while most are ineffective and quickly forgotten. In short, 'sticky' messages have a number of common characteristics, summarised in the mnemonic SUCCES:

- Simple: the core idea is easy to explain and understand, in plain English

- Unexpected: an element of surprise helps the message cut through

- Concrete: the core points or takeaways need to be clear and easily visualised

- Credible: the message needs to be believable, as does the person telling it

- Emotional: the message needs to link to things people care about

- Stories: telling stories helps people remember messages and share them with others.

My Disney story ticked all of these boxes, which is why it had such an impact on staff. And if you want to be an effective communicator, look for stories that bring your messages to life.

Keeping messages simple and memorable takes effort, even though it sounds easy. Aside from (probably) not having had specific business writing training, leaders have to overcome a number of inherent tendencies, including:

- knowing their material and competitive situation in detail

- being conditioned to think about the pros and cons of any issue

- having spent years absorbing industry jargon and 'corporate-speak'.

Using a framework such as SUCCES to plan and develop your messaging can help, as can working with a professional writer or editor who is skilled at boiling messages down to their essence. The more groups you speak to, the more you'll find you can pare back the message to its essence and identify the stories, analogies and phrases that resonate with your people.

In time, cutting out unnecessary words and jargon becomes both a habit and an obsession, as does asking 'what's our made-to-stick point?' The best communicators use punchy, evocative language rather than multisyllabic words and corporate jargon. Remember these quotes?

- 'Mr Gorbachev, tear down this wall' — Ronald Reagan

- 'We choose to go to the moon in this decade, and do the other things, not because they are easy, but because they are hard ...' — John F Kennedy

- 'If you can't feed a team with two pizzas, it's too large' — Jeff Bezos

Whether for internal or external messages, I always challenge myself and my teams to pare the message back to a 'sticky' phrase that leaders can repeat, and teams can remember.

For example:

- a strategy to 'Reduce customer wait time and simplify our product set' became the mantra 'Convenience and simplicity'
- a project to 'Reduce the mortgage origination process time by 90 per cent' became 'the Ten-Minute Mortgage'
- a culture program to improve service quality became 'People helping people'
- a set of 20 service quality commitments became 'The Customer Charter'.

Employees are inundated with messages on a daily basis. Keep it simple, and keep it sticky!

Nonverbal messaging

Finally, it's worth remembering that not all communication is verbal. All of the following actions send messages:

- how you dress
- where, when and how you visit teams
- where you choose to sit and stand in a meeting
- where you eat lunch
- whether you drive, fly or take the bus
- how you respond to customer complaints.

Do you see yourself as one of the team, or above everyone else? Do you walk the floors, or hide out in the Ivory Tower? Do you stand in the coffee queue in the morning, or slip quietly into the executive elevator? Are you easy to approach and genuinely interested in people? Can you take criticism and feedback without getting defensive?

As a leader, you are constantly on show for your people, regardless of your seniority. Your actions easily speak louder than your words, and a few well-chosen symbolic acts will spread like wildfire, particularly if they demonstrate care, a commitment to clearing the way, or an interest in celebrating the organisation's unsung heroes.

As with verbal communication, symbolic acts need to have an element of surprise, sacrifice and emotional impact about them if they're going to stick. For example:

- showing up (with cake) at 2 am to visit a project team working an all-nighter
- greeting staff in the lobby on an important day
- visiting front-line staff in a disaster zone, bringing with you much-needed supplies
- participating in staff fundraising events — fun runs, cycle rides, head shaves, and so on.
- waiting in the coffee queue each morning, and chatting with anyone
- using mass transit rather than driving your own car to a meeting
- removing your suit coat or dressing down appropriately for team visits
- attending welcome and farewell functions for junior staff and retirees
- visiting a seriously ill staff member in hospital
- hosting family days for employees, their partners and children
- joining others' team meetings by video, and sharing a team selfie.

Actions such as these — if done with genuine care and empathy — go a long way to building emotional bonds between leaders and their teams that pay dividends in staff engagement.

If you're the CEO, this is doubly true. Every single thing you say or do is amplified, scrutinised and interpreted. For a normal person who has risen to the role from within the organisation, this can be hard to get your head around — you're still the same person you were, and you assume people know you and where you're coming from. But whether you like it or not, everyone in the organisation now views you through a filter.

This can be a great positive, because your symbolic acts can reach broadly into the organisation. But the downside risks are also large—a loose statement or insensitive gesture when you're tired or distracted can rapidly escalate into a perception that you are upset with something or someone, thereby undoing a lot of good engagement work.

4. Listen, adjust and keep at it

As the saying goes, 'God gave you two ears and one mouth. Use them in those proportions.'

You don't have to be Steve Jobs or a world-class speaker to build high engagement. In fact, I know one executive who is legendary at building highly engaged teams but is actually a pretty poor public speaker. But he is also a world-class listener, with a spooky-good memory for names and faces, whose every word and gesture demonstrates how authentically he cares about people. Over the years he has worked hard to get better at managing his nervous energy and communicating hard messages when he has to.

It's a cliché to say that communications are a two-way street. But sustaining engagement really does require listening closely to understand where people are buying into your messages, and where they're tuning out.

One particular area to watch is differences in audience demographics. For example (while I hate to generalise), engaging effectively with a group of over-60s probably requires more formality and care in your word choice and analogies than does talking to a room full of recent graduates.

On the other hand, as a communications professional friend of mine once observed, it's amazing how often companies ask people to 'go back in time' when they come to work: for example, sending out formal emails that use words and phrases that sound like they were written by Jack Welch, the former CEO of GE, in 1991.

That doesn't mean you should talk down to people or try to be someone you're not—authenticity is still critical. Think of the challenge as like having a radio with a variety of settings—tuning your dial to the appropriate station depending on the audience.

To get better at tuning your dial, it's important to find avenues for unvarnished feedback so you can adjust your messages and delivery to suit your audience. This includes having trusted staff members who can take soundings from influential people throughout the organisation and watching videos of yourself giving presentations or conducting meetings (trust me — it's painful, but incredibly helpful).

It's also useful to collect feedback through paper or email surveys at the end of important presentations, as well as through comments on internal social media, to see which messages stuck and what people intend to do differently as a consequence.

A great mentor once said to me that good communications are about delivering messages in a way that they connect with the listener's values, rather than your own. You can't do that if you're not curious and listening to know how your people feel, and what's important to them. So, keep at it — if you're genuine in your intent and care, people will notice.

A note on communications professionals

Large organisations often have dedicated communications teams to help in developing communications plans, drafting messages and giving feedback on what works and what doesn't.

If you do have access to dedicated communications support, whether from internal or external professionals, there are a few points to bear in mind:

- own the content
- edit it yourself
- maintain your judgement.

First, you have to own the content. While the best communications people know the business well, they are unlikely to know its challenges and subtleties as well as you do. It's simply not fair or realistic to ask a junior communications person to develop a fully formed engagement plan on their own — it has to reflect your own personal values and beliefs.

Second, you need to take an interest in the writing and editing of your messages. Sadly, many communications professionals quickly revert to writing corporate-speak, in part to make up for their lack of content knowledge. It can be time-consuming and painful, but personally editing your important communications to remove jargon is worth the effort when employees feel that they are really hearing from you.

Finally, you have to maintain your judgement on the balance between employee engagement and commercial objectives. Leadership inevitably means making difficult and unpopular decisions, and most people see through spin. It's better to build trust by speaking plainly and calling a spade a spade. This reduces the amount of second-guessing and mistrust that's created in a culture when people suspect they aren't hearing the whole truth.

When times are tough, people judge leaders by whether they are out walking the halls and explaining their decisions or hiding behind an anonymous corporate message. (For an example of how to deliver a tough message while re-affirming the corporate values, see the memo Brian Chesky, CEO of Airbnb, sent on 5 May 2020 to his employees — and published online — announcing significant layoffs as a result of the damage done to their business by the coronavirus.)

A good communications team also serves as an important two-way channel for leaders:

- helping bring important facts to the fore
- calling out managerial spin or wishful thinking when they see it
- anticipating concerns that people will have
- making sure that employees have access to communication channels with the next level of detail.

You now have all the knowledge you need to build engagement in most normal situations that a leader will face. But occasionally as a leader you may find yourself in times of crisis, where the approach to engagement needs to be adjusted to reflect the circumstances. In the next chapter we look at a few of these examples and offer some techniques to build or maintain engagement in times of stress and crisis.

COMMUNICATE

Summary

Effective and continuous communications are critical to demonstrating each of the five points in the Leadership Star. You simply can't rely on a few one-off presentations and emails to build engagement—communications are central to the engaging leader's role. Your goal needs to be to get people talking and engaging with you and each other so that the highly engaged culture you're after takes on a life of its own.

Key points:

- Build a structured communication plan and embed it in your diary.

- Use multiple channels to target different stakeholder groups over time.

- Design messages that stick: Simple, Unexpected, Concrete, Credible, Emotional Stories (SUCCES). Find your own 'Disney' stories, and keep telling them.

- Remember that your actions speak louder than your words.

- Keep at it—show you care by listening more than talking.

Questions for reflection

- How structured is my communications program? How much time do I spend on it through the year? Is it in my calendar?

- Who are my stakeholders and how often do I need to connect with them?

- Am I using all the informal and formal communication channels available to me?

- What is the one thing I need to work on as a presenter? As a writer?

- How 'sticky' are my messages? What stories do I tell on a regular basis? Do employees remember those stories and the key points? Do they say them back to me, and to others?

- How do I know that my messages are getting through, and not being filtered?

- How do I know how people are reacting to my messages? Are they hearing what I intend?

- How do I know that I'm hearing the truth about what is going on?

- When is the last time I walked the floors on my own and spoke to junior people without their boss in the room? What did I learn, and how did I respond?

- When is the last time someone in my team raised a real concern with me? How did I react? What was the resolution? Did I follow through personally, or did I delegate it?

ENGAGEMENT IN TIMES OF CRISIS

The 80 people who squashed into the drab conference room did not look happy.

Several of them stood with their arms folded, openly sceptical looks (or was it anger?) on their faces. At least a quarter of the room stared at the floor, occasionally glancing in my direction. A few looked shell-shocked. The rest just looked at me blankly.

I had landed in Singapore that morning, flying overnight from London, and had come straight to the office to address the staff in this outpost of an international private bank. On the previous Thursday, we'd learned that the local managing director and all of his senior staff had defected to a rival Swiss bank.

Staff engagement, which had been persistently low in this business due to a litany of staff complaints, was now all but shattered. Competitors were circling our best bankers, hoping to steal them and our customers away. I didn't know any of the people well, having taken responsibility for the division in which this business sat only two months previously.

To top it all off, the executive who had led this business for several years — one of my direct reports — didn't think the situation was urgent enough to warrant flying out with me. So aside from a couple of remaining long-term managers, I was alone at the front of the room, working desperately to salvage a situation I didn't create.

What could I say to these people to buy some time and get things back on track?

Up to this point in the book I've assumed that your organisation has some level of stability that allows you to focus on one or two aspects of the Leadership Star while executing a comprehensive engagement plan over time. Earning trust and building engagement both take time, and that's especially true in a large organisation where your role spans more than one layer of management.

From time to time, however, you will face situations that *aren't* stable or predictable — for example, during:

- the startup phase of a business
- financial hardship, a cash flow crisis or bankruptcy
- mergers, takeovers or significant technology or process changes
- external reputational, legal or regulatory challenges
- significant leadership changes or personnel upheaval
- environmental disasters, pandemics or public safety/terrorism incidents.

Over my 30-year career in banking I've had to navigate my fair share of crises, including:

- economic recessions
- large credit and fraud losses
- the Global Financial Crisis
- failed-company turnarounds, acquisitions and divestitures
- reputational crises
- poor senior executive conduct

- leadership team defections

- board governance crises

- major technology outages, service breakdowns and labour disputes

- terrorism, cyber-security events, hold-ups, kidnappings, protestor sit-ins and overseas coups

- earthquakes, floods, tsunamis, volcanoes, hurricanes, bushfires and a pandemic

- direct political interventions

- regulatory and class-action lawsuits

- a Banking Royal Commission and a regulatory compliance crisis that ultimately cost me my job.

Based on these experiences, this chapter offers suggestions about how the Leadership Star framework can be adapted to help you keep your team engaged and effective during periods of great stress and change.

This is *not* a comprehensive approach to leadership in times of crisis — that's a much bigger topic. But focusing on four key elements of leadership can make a big difference to maintaining (or even increasing) engagement during these times. Specifically:

1. lay the groundwork

2. recognise changing needs

3. communicate with empathy

4. be decisive.

1. Lay the groundwork

Rebuilding or sustaining engagement in challenging times is a lot about resilience — specifically, your employees' resilience in the face of stress and uncertainty.

It is much easier to build resilience when people have a basic sense of security than when their assumptions about the world have been turned upside down, they feel powerless to control their own destiny, or they've lost hope in the future.

Demonstrating Care, providing Context and giving Clarity each help build resilience to stress and change. But to prepare people for potential crises it's particularly important to provide Context that reminds people that the future is uncertain and manages their expectations about how and (how quickly) their world can change.

Let me share a personal example.

When the unexpected regulatory and reputational issues that led to my departure from Westpac emerged, several members of my team commented on how surprisingly calm I seemed in the face of such a potentially severe setback to my career and reputation. The reason for this, I explained, was that I always understood that this could happen when you are CEO.

The privilege of leadership comes with accountability — I may not have caused the issue, but as the CEO I owned it. I had emotionally prepared for this by reminding myself of this fact and having a list of things for me to do in the future if it did.

Because I had prepared in this way, when it did happen I was able to remain calm and focused on what actions we needed to take to fix the issue, rather than becoming paralysed with shock and fear about what it meant for me.

For an organisation more broadly, being upfront with people about potential changes, challenges and risks can similarly prepare them to stay focused and constructive when they do emerge.

What would you do if ...

One good way to do this is through scenario planning exercises. Have your leadership team brainstorm all the potential surprises that could hit your organisation, and then make a point of actually role-playing your way through a few of those surprises on a regular basis:

- If this happens, what would we do?
- Who would be responsible for doing what?

- What else could go wrong in the middle of this scenario, and what would we do then?

- What choices would we have to make, and how would we make them?

- How would we communicate to our employees and stakeholders?

By practising your crisis response in as real a situation as possible, your team will become calmer and more prepared to think clearly and provide stable leadership when a situation does arise. And at the same time, you'll identify specific steps — stockpiling supplies, locking up partnership support, pre-drafting standard communications and checklists — that will help you reduce the impact of many situations, even if you can't fully predict the nature of what will hit you.

For example, the COVID-19 pandemic highlighted the benefit of this pre-work in banks: although the global nature of the economic shutdown wasn't expected, the strength of Australian banks' capital positions and speed of launching customer assistance packages was a direct result of scenarios that had been war-gamed by bank leadership teams in the preceding years.

Leave a trail of breadcrumbs

'Breadcrumbs' or 'trial balloons' are another way to help manage an organisation through periods of rapid change or stress. If you are upfront with people about the challenges the organisation is facing, and some of the changes that may need to be made, it gives people time to process so that, when final changes are announced, the amount of shock is reduced. This helps people think more clearly about the changes — in some cases they may actually experience a sense of relief.

Some leaders will find this approach too indirect and prefer to be blunt in their change messages. And in times of crisis it may well be that delivering a shock is a better way of driving rapid change. From an engagement point of view, however, it's definitely worth laying the groundwork upfront — 'dropping breadcrumbs' — so that your people approach change with a more confident and secure mindset.

2. Recognise changing needs

Employees' needs and priorities change over time, reflecting both their own personal situation and the organisation's internal dynamics. For example, the priorities and motivations of a single mother working in a high-pressure sales environment are likely to be quite different than those of a well-paid executive who is one step away from a large corporation's C-suite.

Maslow's hierarchy of needs (see figure 8.1) provides a useful way to think about this dynamic. Maslow argued that an individual's motivations rise step by step from physiological and safety needs (food, water, security) through psychological needs (relationships, love, prestige) and finally to 'self-actualisation' (achieving one's full potential). Only once the lower needs are met does the individual's focus rise to the next level.

From an engagement perspective, the more one's basic physical and psychological needs are met, the more that higher-order priorities such as pride and creative expression become the way to motivate people. Conversely, if basic needs are threatened, higher-order priorities fall away and motivational drivers return to meeting basic needs.

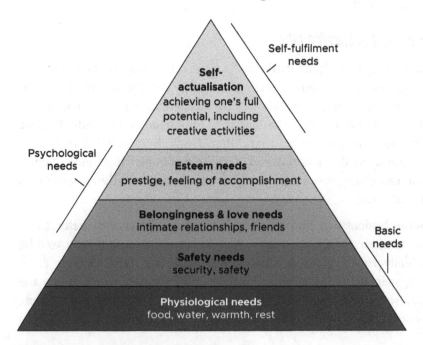

Figure 8.1: Maslow's hierarchy of needs

In times of uncertainty or crisis, people are likely to experience the issue as threatening to needs that they haven't worried about for a while — and this creates anxiety that can manifest in both strange behaviour and a loss of motivation.

The nature of the change often creates challenges to general employees that don't affect the leader in the same way. More senior people may be more financially secure, have a safe and supportive home life, and have enough experience and contacts to not have to worry about finding another job.

So, it's critical that leaders in these situations take time to identify how different groups and individuals may be experiencing the change, so that the steps they take will genuinely resonate with the people affected.

For example, in Australia the annual bushfire and cyclone seasons often wreak havoc in regional areas, destroying lives, homes and livelihoods — while leaving most urban areas relatively unaffected. Bank employees living in regional areas are often affected in multiple ways — both as residents whose homes, families and friends are at risk, and as bankers trying to help anguished customers get back on their feet.

I'll never forget some of the actions great leaders in my team took during natural disasters. In one case, a regional manager drove five hours to deliver a car full of dry towels to staff in a cyclone-affected area. (It was their top request: the branch and everyone in it was soaked.) In another, staff from branches in an unaffected part of the state drove to a bushfire area to provide work relief to their colleagues, so that they could leave work and tend to their own damaged homes.

It's relatively straightforward to identify how needs change during a natural disaster or a major security incident such as a war or terrorist attack. But sometimes the impact of change is subtler, and leaders have to work harder to identify it.

As I write, the world is still grappling with the dangers and uncertainties of the COVID-19 pandemic. In this environment, organisations that can provide job security to employees with a mortgage or other substantial commitments may find that loyalty and motivation actually increase despite reductions in pay and other forms of recognition.

This dynamic reflects another important insight about human psychology: happiness is largely a *relative* game. Leaders can help both engagement and their people's emotional wellbeing by positioning the organisation's current challenges in a broader relative perspective — such as, by pointing out where others face even greater challenges. Similarly, encouraging people to practise gratitude on a regular basis has been shown to improve happiness in people facing stressful situations.[1]

Some people will *always* find change difficult, if not personally threatening. Young and ambitious employees may be excited about the growth opportunities created by a new function or business division, viewing change as likely to give them a chance to prove themselves. However, the same announcement may be quite scary to someone who knows they have risen as far as they can go in the organisation, and whose personal financial obligations mean that they can't afford to lose their job. That person is unlikely to come clean about their motivation and may instead resort to fighting the change in a variety of overt and covert ways.

3. Communicate with empathy

Chapter 7 covers how important authentic communications are to deliver and reinforce each aspect of the Leadership Star. In times of crisis, this is critical.

When the situation is uncertain, it can be tempting for leaders to go to ground or to focus purely on the urgent commercial aspects of their situation. Often decisions need to be made and communicated quickly. Leaders may not believe they have time to provide much context or to worry about people's feelings — they need to act.

Facing the brutal reality and focusing on the issues at hand is good practice for leaders in times like this. But that doesn't mean you can't — or shouldn't — make time to communicate frequently to your people.

Miriam, whose story I share in chapter 1, once shared with me a great insight about how she prepared for the very stressful meeting where she

---

[1] See, for example, health.harvard.edu, 'Giving thanks can make you happier', and 'How gratitude changes you and your brain', Joel Wong and Joshua Brown, *Greater Good Magazine*.

announced that we were closing the Hong Kong credit card business. 'I was very stressed out about it ... but then I realised that my stress was mostly about me looking bad,' she told me. 'I didn't want to look like a bad person to my team.

'But then I realised that this wasn't about me. And I was selfish. My job as a leader was not to justify this but to be there for them. My role as a leader is to be of service to others.'

In a crisis, this means giving people strength and hope to carry on, as well as the belief that the effort is worth it.

Providing a flow of clear, authentic and empathetic communications can go a long way to helping your people process what is happening and respond in a constructive way, rather than shutting down or devolving into political or defensive self-preservation.

Specifically, there are four elements of an effective message in difficult times:

1. Tell it straight.
2. Tell it with empathy.
3. Put actions in context.
4. Give people some control.

Tell it straight

You may not have all the answers. That's okay. As clearly as you can, state:

- what you do know
- what you don't know
- why you think it happened (if you know)
- what work is under way to get to the bottom of it
- what people can expect next, and over what time frame.

Tell it with empathy

Acknowledge how people are feeling: 'I know it's hard/disappointing. I recognise that you have also been dealing with X or Y. I know this is tough to deal with.' Acknowledge—to the extent you can say it authentically—that this is painful or difficult for you too.

Put actions in context

Remind people of the organisation's higher purpose, and the organisation's ongoing commitment to that purpose. Explain what steps are being taken and their rationale. Build emotional commitment by showing how those steps link to purpose and values: 'Here's what we're going to do, and here's why that is consistent with what we believe in.'

It can also be helpful to put your team's situation in *relative* context by reminding them of colleagues, competitors or community members who are facing similar (or worse) challenges and demonstrating your own gratitude for the relative position you are in or options that you have.

Give people some control

Powerlessness, or the inability to exercise any influence over what is happening to us, is deeply unsettling in times of crisis. Show people how they can exert an influence—however small—over the potential outcomes:

- What actions can they each take?
- How can they share their ideas or provide feedback on what is being done?
- What choices can they make?

Empathetic communication in action

For a real-life example of putting this framework into practice, let's return to that unhappy conference room in Singapore.

Standing at the front of the room, with no podium, no slides and no notes, I said:

Good morning everyone. I'm glad to finally get here to Singapore but I'm sorry that my first visit had to be in such difficult circumstances.

In addition to the local CEO, we've lost five senior executives and several of our top relationship bankers. I also know that several of you have been approached by our competitors and many of you are wondering whether you want to stay here as well.

Before I talk about what we're going to do, I want you to know that I know you've been through a really tough time, not just last week but over the last couple of years. With all the challenges the bank has faced in the financial crisis, there's been a real question about whether we're still committed to investing in this business, and to whether we want to keep our international offices at all.

Just looking at the state of this office, I can see that there's been a clear lack of investment in both the working environment and the technology that you use. I'm sure that's been very frustrating and has taken a toll on all of you.

I also want you to know that from my standpoint this situation is really disappointing. It should never have been allowed to get to this point. Being new to the bank, I'm really frustrated on your behalf at my management team and I'm going to fix it.

To be honest, I don't know yet what that means exactly. That's why I wanted to come here in person — so you could hear from me directly that we're committed to fixing it, and for me to hear from you about what issues you think we need to address. I can't promise I can fix every issue you've got, because the reality is that the world has changed after the financial crisis.

I do know, however, that our starting point is good: for the past three hundred years, our brand has stood for delivering great service to families through the generations — not just making short-term trades to maximise our revenue. That makes our brand a great asset in a crowded market and defines the kind of bankers we want to work here. As a result, we have some fantastic and loyal customers, and a number of longstanding employees who really care about this place. That's a solid foundation for a good business, and for great career opportunities over time.

I know it's been frustrating, but each of you can help make this a great place again by being patient, by not making any rash decisions, by sharing your thoughts and suggestions with me, and by focusing your effort externally on looking after our customers well — because they're hurting too.

That's all I wanted to say for now — and thank you for listening and for hanging in there. Let's open it up for your observations and your questions.

So, did it work?

Six years after this meeting the bank decided to sell all of its offshore private banking, including the Singapore office, to a (different) Swiss-based competitor. But the Singapore business was still there, and significantly improved from the dire state left by its previous management.

In the immediate aftermath of the defection, a relatively small number of staff left, but most stayed. Most senior leaders were replaced, the technology system was modernised, and the office was moved to a modern building with great customer facilities. The brand was relaunched to the market, high-quality bankers joined, high-potential staff were promoted and engagement improved dramatically.

I'll never forget the tension in the room that day, and have no doubt that an immediate, well-structured, authentic and empathetic conversation with the staff headed off what could have been a terminal disaster for the business.

4. Be decisive

As a leader, you strive to make good decisions — your credibility, and your team's trust in you, depend on it. And you probably know that making good judgements depends on taking time to source data, seek diverse perspectives and carefully weigh the consequences of different options.

Sometimes this means having the confidence not to rush an important decision. But in times of crisis or great change, giving people clarity and certainty takes precedence, even if means occasionally reversing course.

The human need for control over one's environment is quite fundamental. And when a period of instability undermines that sense of control, people look to their leaders to restore that control and predictability.

Unfortunately, during a crisis the fear of making a poor judgement can trap leaders in analysis paralysis or a futile search for consensus.

From an engagement perspective, this lack of clarity can easily cascade into organisational paralysis, poor execution and a demotivated workforce — at a time when you need exactly the opposite.

Several areas in particular where it's important to move quickly are:

- leadership changes
- clarity of authority and accountability
- investment and resource decisions
- performance targets.

Leadership changes

In normal times, you may wish to plan leadership changes carefully, for example allowing a dignified exit for an under-performer. In crisis, speed is essential and rapid leadership change is sometimes required to help the organisation rebuild. (In my Singapore story, for example, the senior leader who failed to make the trip was quickly exited.) Be careful about unfair scapegoating, however, as the perception that senior management are simply protecting their own positions can quickly undermine staff trust.

Clarity of authority and accountability

Matrix management can slow down decision making as it cascades through an organisation. In crisis it is essential that individual leaders are given the authority to cut through and make decisions, even at the risk of upsetting internal stakeholders.

Changes in accountability and authority must also be clearly communicated — any short-term ego-bruising that this causes will be more than made up for by the broader organisation's sense that important decisions are being made. Symbolic acts such as daily leadership meetings, where key decisions are communicated more broadly, can also help instil confidence across the organisation.

Investment and resource decisions

As with the previous point, accelerating investment, divestment and other resource decisions (for example, significant headcount reductions or staff redeployment) is a good way to demonstrate that leaders are on the case.

Bear in mind that not everyone will like the choices — so be sure to clearly communicate the rationale for what *doesn't* get done, as well as what *does*. People may not like the decisions, but if they understand and accept the rationale, they will usually stay neutral-to-positive and supportive of the leadership with their own teams.

Performance targets

Somewhat ironically, setting tougher performance or activity targets can be a useful way to sustain engagement during tough times. This is essentially about taking Clarity up a notch — minimising the number of things you ask people to do, while increasing the amount of stretch that you bake into the goals.

Provided the goals don't seem capricious or lacking in integrity, they can create a 'war-time' mentality that binds people together emotionally, as well as channelling people's energy into productive activity and away from wallowing in engagement-killing despair.

Special situations

Full-blown crises aren't the only unusual situation you may face from an engagement perspective. So before leaving this chapter, here are a few engagement tips related to specific situations that you may face:

- startups
- mergers, acquisitions and divestments
- human crises
- behavioural, ethical or reputational crises
- a crisis of success.

Startups

By definition, startups can't promise the same stability or career progression that established companies can, and typically have fairly immature HR programs and departments. And with costs under pressure, they often can't pay salaries that are as attractive as those offered by larger companies in mature markets. As a consequence, many startup leaders gravitate to a low-probability, high-payoff compensation scheme to attract and retain their people — essentially dangling the prospect of owning shares in the next Google, Amazon, Tesla or Uber.

While the prospect of potential riches can create a highly motivated workforce, its staying power is fragile: a few missed market milestones or failed capital raisings and the best people may quickly run for the exits.

That's why providing Context in particular is so essential for startup leaders. By framing the business's purpose as trying to solve a meaningful problem for society or a particular customer need, startup leaders give their employees reasons to feel committed that go beyond the financial rewards. And by taking the time to define and commit to a particular set of values and behaviours, the organisation can more easily attract a group of like-minded people who work effectively together and enjoy each other's company — a further psychic reward.

Startups give leaders the ability to start with a blank sheet of paper in terms of their goals, values, culture and forms of recognition; plus, a relatively small team means that demonstrating care and communicating the other aspects of the Leadership Star is more logistically straightforward than in a large corporation.

Mergers, acquisitions and divestments

While 'cultural fit' is often acknowledged as critical in mergers, leaders can become so focused on completing the transaction that they overlook practical steps that can maintain engagement during the period.

Changes in business ownership create significant uncertainty for people on both sides of the potential transaction. Acquired or divested staff may worry about losing their jobs, while those on the acquiring side may fear changes in responsibilities or reporting lines once the deal is complete. Managers on the acquiring side sometimes don't exercise sufficient empathy in their dealings with the opposite side, while those on either side of the transaction may act disrespectfully towards the other — embedding ongoing resentment.

The best staff on both sides of the transaction may decide to leave or at least become vulnerable to recruitment by rival firms. And widespread disaffection among staff can lead to a drop in productivity or service quality that threatens the very rationale for the deal.

Some of the best practices to help offset these traps include:

- *Over-communicating:* malicious rumours spread rapidly in a vacuum. Use regular briefings to allow people to ask questions and invite people to share rumours they've heard so you can address them. Be as transparent as you can — people can handle bad news if it's delivered honestly and empathetically. It's okay not to have all the answers or to have some information that can't be shared, but consistent briefings over time help calm people's fear of the unknown. This includes communicating regularly with unions and other sources of information that people will look to so that messages are consistent.

- *Being clear about time frames and process:* reduce uncertainty by helping people know *when* and *how* key decisions will be made. For example, it may be that job losses aren't going to be determined for several months; giving people a view on the time frame and process by which this will be determined can help them re-focus on the task at hand and possibly even motivate them to perform better in advance of an upcoming evaluation process.

- *Making people decisions quickly:* internal political battles can be incredibly negative for engagement and poisonous to organisational culture. The sooner key appointments are made, the sooner the new leaders can refocus on engaging their teams.

- *Resolving differences in terms and conditions:* when people are feeling vulnerable, small things can make a big difference to their motivation. Variations in terms and conditions — changes in leave entitlements, reductions in effective pay, undesirable office moves or the loss of a symbolic perk — can rapidly escalate into widespread disaffection. Each situation is different, and organisations need to judge the most effective way to bring together a culture. But it's worth identifying upfront whether symbolic sticking points can be resolved constructively.

- *Implementing targeted retention:* offering targeted financial incentives can be effective at retaining and motivating staff who are key to successful integration or performance during a merger or wind-down period. It's also worth considering whether a broader, shared bonus of some sort — even if relatively small — can be used to help staff see their interests as aligned with the broader deal rationale. More broadly, mergers give leaders the chance to recognise high performers on either side of the transaction through high-profile integration roles, new responsibilities or the chance to lead larger teams.

- *Offering graceful (and generous) exits:* in any divestment or cost-focused integration, it is inevitable that some people will lose their jobs. From an engagement standpoint, the way you handle the people who leave can have a big impact on the ones who stay. Going above and beyond to help people find new roles or get career counselling, being sensitive to difficult health or family situations in timing, and celebrating people's contribution through an appropriate farewell are all things that send an important message of integrity and care to the ones left behind. While it might seem commercially unnecessary, skimping on these factors can quickly undermine engagement, the respect that employees have for their leaders and their commitment to the organisation.

Human crises

Unexpected illnesses, death, family tragedies and environmental disasters are all moments of truth for leaders that can make a lasting impact on a team's performance and motivation. Human nature means that in times of crisis people look to their leaders — especially very senior leaders — for guidance and reassurance, meaning that your actions take on an extra level of symbolic impact. Empathy and authenticity are therefore just as important as a calm focus on what practically needs to be done.

In a 'human' crisis, demonstrating genuine care for your people is critical. This includes moving quickly to address staff safety issues and communicating your personal response to the issues — including being willing to show your own vulnerability and emotional response to tragedy.

To show you mean it, remember to keep checking in after the first rush of the issue: the human toll of a bushfire on a family that's lost its home continues long after the fire is out and the emergency workers have gone.

Symbolic acts such as formally putting people issues at the top of meeting agendas, visiting or phoning the people affected, sending flowers or useful gifts, and providing policy or financial flexibility all send a positive message of commitment to your people that is likely to be reciprocated by the broader employee base.

With this as a foundation, you are better prepared to sustain engagement through difficult situations that have genuine business impacts as well as human impacts — COVID-19 and the related downturn being an obvious example. While situations like this create enormous uncertainty and stress for employees, authentically acknowledging the issue and being willing to share your own personal reactions can help people feel supported through the crisis.

Each situation will be different: the COVID-19 pandemic brought unforeseen challenges to families with school-aged children, shared child custody arrangements, elder care responsibilities and financial dependence on industries or regions that have been battered by shutdowns. Coping with ever-shifting health regulations and advice takes a toll over time. Finding and vetting good people takes longer, team relationships are harder to establish remotely and staring at multi-person Zoom calls all day takes a toll.

These challenges — and others we haven't anticipated yet — require compassion, creativity, flexibility and forward thinking. For leaders, it means thinking carefully about each of your people and your various stakeholder groups and finding new solutions that help each individual get through the crisis.

Over time, putting Care at the top of your crisis response can mean that crises actually increase engagement — since they give employees an opportunity to 'show what sort of people we are'.

Behavioural, ethical or reputational crises

Occasionally, organisations find themselves in the midst of a self-inflicted crisis that can deeply rock the foundations of employee engagement.

Criminal activities, ethical or moral failures, staff misconduct, managerial bullying or discrimination, significant product failures, major compliance breaches or poor customer treatment are all examples of failings that have shattered both the external and internal reputations of prominent organisations in finance, manufacturing, retail, technology, the not-for-profit sector, government and even the military.

While each situation is different, there are three aspects to an effective response from an engagement perspective:

1. respond swiftly and proportionately

2. re-focus your messaging on providing context

3. be patient and consistent.

Respond swiftly and proportionately

While it is important to be thorough and fair, people need to see that the sort of issue that has emerged won't be tolerated — and speed of action is one of the key symbols people will look for. Make no mistake — people will be talking about whatever the issue is, so addressing it head on and publicly is important. If that means the individual involved or leader of an area needs to go or be stood down temporarily, then do it quickly: sometimes a change in leadership is required to show that senior management is committed to fixing the issue.

Re-focus your messaging on providing context

Talk about how serious the issue is, and how you personally feel about it. Then help people understand how and why it happened. People will want to know whether the issue is symptomatic of deeper problems or values issues in the organisation — which might make them re-assess their commitment — or a more specific issue that can be addressed. Also, be sure to show people how the actions you are taking to deal with the issue are consistent with the values and purpose that they already know about the organisation.

Be patient and consistent

As Warren Buffett famously said, 'it takes 20 years to build a reputation, and five minutes to ruin it'. Refocus people on values and purpose. Help them find satisfaction in what they can control, rather than what is said externally. Lay out a plan to understand and address any fundamental problems and execute the plan with great discipline. Over time, look for positive steps you can take to *demonstrate* 'we've changed', building up a set of proof points in the minds of employees and key stakeholders that eventually shifts the narrative.

A crisis of success

Engagement challenges aren't limited to when things go badly — success can bring engagement traps of its own.

Success is generally a positive for engagement: having 'runs on the board' breeds confidence, pride and a willingness to take on new challenges. Good people from outside the organisation are attracted to success and join, resulting in a positive loop of engagement and success.

But when an organisation does well over an extended period of time, its leaders may begin to think that it will continue forever. But complacency brings great dangers: leaders may not pay as much attention to communicating with junior staff or nurturing relationships with colleagues in other parts of the organisation on whom they depend.

Over time, long-serving leaders may start to 'pick their spots' and manage more by exception than by applying consistent discipline across the organisation. This can lead to them delegating or even neglecting areas that are seemingly in good shape, allowing those areas to deteriorate if the manager to whom they have delegated isn't sufficiently across the detail.

Likewise, successful leaders may start to take for granted the quality of their processes or the skills and professionalism of the leaders who work for them. In some cases, this failure to 'inspect what you expect' can allow problems to grow unnoticed in previously well-performing areas. And since organisations turn over their staff on average every three to six years, a lack of continued discipline on each aspect of the Leadership Star means the foundations of engagement can quickly slip away.

Organisations that pride themselves on being a meritocracy can also miss the role that good luck or good timing can often have on results for a business or individual. If this is allowed to develop into an us-versus-them, internally competitive culture, long-term engagement and retention of key people are likely to suffer.

Some level of internal competition is healthy to drive people to be their best. But leaders who care about long-term engagement make a clear distinction between driving yourself and the organisation to be the best and competing and winning against an *external* adversary.

The best way to sustain engagement in a successful organisation is to constantly reinforce to people that what got you here won't get you there. In other words, provide context that reminds people how luck and other factors have contributed to success so far, and how that context is changing and creating new opportunities for growth and challenges to overcome.

Give people clarity on how the bar is lifting on what constitutes world-class performance.

By all means, build pride by celebrating success, but then find a way to draw a line for people and re-focus them on the future. If it helps, use analogies from sports or other disciplines to make the point: Michael Jordan, Serena Williams, Steve Jobs, Christine Lagarde and the Rolling Stones didn't get to where they are by being satisfied with their early achievements. As Roger Federer said after winning his sixteenth Grand Slam in 2010, 'There's still a lot to play for. But usually if you stay the same, you will move down. That's never something I was content with.'

Cross-cultural engagement

The Singapore story at the start of this chapter has one other aspect that is worth bearing in mind when thinking about applying the Leadership Star framework: how to address cultural or language differences when building engagement. While I'm by no means familiar with all the ways in which cultural differences can manifest themselves in different organisations, I have overseen businesses in multiple countries and continents, and drawn a few conclusions that you may find helpful.

My first observation is an obvious one: deep down, people are people. They all love their families and come to work hoping to do a good job and be recognised for their contribution. They are each animated by a mix of pride, aspiration, loyalty and fear, and generally mean well. In this respect, the five points of the Leadership Star — Care, Context, Clarity, Clear the way and Celebrate — apply everywhere.

When managing across various languages and cultures, however, there are a number of subtleties that are worth bearing in mind:

- different feedback styles
- local nuances
- cultural values.

Different feedback styles

The first is the way in which people provide feedback. Understanding how people are feeling is fundamental to engagement, but in some cultures you'll never get straight feedback from staff, especially in a public forum. They may consider it an inappropriate place to give feedback, lack confidence in their public speaking or English language skills, be afraid of losing face, or the culture may instil respect for senior people that means one never challenges them. At best, you may get some 'softball' questions that imply a comment or perspective.

In these situations, it's important to take multiple soundings — through one-on-one or small group meetings, building relationships with respected influencers deep in the organisation, and offering anonymous surveys or whistleblowing lines. External consultants, business partners and regulators can also be useful sources of insight. You can't expect to simply run a town hall session and know for sure what people are feeling.

The opposite can be true as well — some cultures thrive on conflict and like nothing better than to throw 'fastballs' at a new leader in a public forum. This can be particularly true when someone looks or sounds different from the group, or when you're going into an inherently hostile situation such as a restructure or a takeover. In these situations, I always tried not to take the aggression personally, acknowledge the underlying emotion behind the point being made, and then clarify and respond as best I could — politely but firmly pushing back where necessary. You don't earn respect — and engagement — from your people by rolling over at the first sign of conflict.

Local nuances

The second subtlety is the importance of demonstrating respect for local nuance.

The first time I visited Tasmania, I remember the regional manager who picked me up waxing lyrical about the differences between north and south Tasmania. When I commented on how nice the area that we were driving through was, he said, 'Well, sure, but this is *north* of the Hobart River. Now, *south* of the Hobart River is a lot nicer ...'

Everywhere I've travelled in my career, across multiple continents and countries — north, south, east and west — I've always been told the same thing: 'It's different here.'

In other words, people are always proud of something that distinguishes where they live. Find out what it is, and make a point of acknowledging it, publicly. It might be something about the food, or local beer. Maybe it's an aspect of the lifestyle, religion, art or music. Maybe it's an aspect of sport (hint: in New Zealand, it rhymes with 'haul back'). To find out, read the local papers, and ask people what's topical in the local news and what they're looking forward to doing on the weekend.

This also applies to language and pronunciation. People won't necessarily expect you to speak the local language, but it helps if you make an effort, especially around totemic people, things and holidays ('Gong xi fa cai!'). At a minimum, learn to pronounce the name of the city properly (hint for my American friends: it's 'Melbuhn', not 'Mell-born').

Making an effort sends two important messages to employees: 'I get it' and 'I respect you.' As a leader from another jurisdiction, your words and actions will inevitably be judged through a double stereotype: as a representative of your own culture, and as someone from HQ. Demonstrating you 'get' and respect what's different about a place helps put people at ease and lowers their guard so that your broader messages can get through.

Cultural values

A final note about culture. As a Western company operating in a non-Western environment, you may occasionally be confronted with assertions that don't line up with your or your organisation's values—for example, in treatment of women; people of different caste, race, religion or sexual preferences; or in the willingness to pay bribes. You may be told that certain things that wouldn't be acceptable in your home country are okay or expected there.

Don't buy into it.

While you must respect and obey local laws and be sensitive to local culture, compromising fundamental values does not serve you in the long term. For one thing, sticking with Western values and standards of behaviour may be the very reason why people want to join your organisation rather than a local one in the first place. And becoming known locally for giving people a chance to thrive in an organisation that judges them based on their contribution rather than who they are is a great way for a foreign company to attract great people, build their loyalty and drive engagement.

ENGAGEMENT IN TIMES OF CRISIS

Summary

Not all situations that you'll face as a leader will give you the luxury of designing and rolling out a long-term engagement plan.

In crisis, the Leadership Star provides a useful reference for helping you lead people through in ways that keep them motivated and engaged.

Crisis is when the fundamental points of the Leadership Star are at their most important:

- demonstrating Care for people who feel uncertain
- providing Context to help people to evaluate what's happening to them, and what you're asking them to do
- giving them Clarity about the actions they can take to control or at least influence their own destiny
- Clearing away confusion and obstacles to staying motivated and engaged
- building retention and loyalty by Celebrating a high performer's success with financial incentives and new opportunities for growth.

Crises tend to reveal your true character, and learning from crisis will help you become the best leader you can be.

Crises can be stressful, frightening, disappointing and rewarding for a leader. But as we discuss in the conclusion that follows, there are few rewards more satisfying than successfully leading your people through tough times.

Questions for reflection

- When have I been most challenged in my personal and professional life? What did I learn about myself?

- Have I and my team prepared for potential crises that may come? If not, what more should we do to anticipate and practise what we'll do when they come?

- How can I best serve my people in this moment?

- What character traits do I want to demonstrate in a crisis? What personal 'dark sides' do I need to avoid?

- How will I manage my energy to sustain myself through the challenges ahead?

- What am I most personally afraid of? What's the worst that could happen, and what steps can I take now to prepare myself for that possibility?

CONCLUSION

Leadership is never a sure thing. There's no one formula that will guarantee your success, despite what all the gurus and celebrity CEOs tell you. The strategic and operational disciplines necessary to build and grow a business are quite different from those needed to revive a business in trouble. External changes, crises and disruptions can knock your business off course. The larger your organisation, and the more senior you are, the more individual errors can compound on your watch before you even know about them.

But you can tip the odds in your favour. A high-quality, highly engaged workforce, aligned around a clear purpose and set of values, is much more likely to compete effectively. And a caring, open culture, with leaders at all levels who demonstrate that it's safe to speak up, is more likely to highlight issues before they become fatal.

Leaders who build highly engaged teams attract high performers to join those teams, setting up a virtuous spiral of engagement and performance. For me, that's what leadership is ultimately about — creating the conditions that allow you to achieve as a team.

And while there are no guarantees, a leader who is authentic and disciplined about living and communicating each point of the Leadership Star — and expects their team members to do the same with *their* teams — gives themselves an excellent chance at building and sustaining high engagement over time.

The Leadership Star framework is deliberately simple. Five points, each starting with C, making it easy to memorise. (While I'd be delighted if you refer back to this book from time to time, I've tried to write it in a way that's so easy to remember that you won't have to.)

Let's recap the five things you personally need to do as a leader to build engagement.

First, and most importantly, to Care — about each of your people as individuals, rather than as a collective notion that 'I care about my people'. Care also means caring about *outcomes*, not just *process* — showing people that the quality of their work matters, and that you're prepared to use direct feedback and tough love where needed to help people be their best. And remember too that care is an action verb — you have to show you care through the way you interact with people, the decisions you make and the steps you take. Remember Miriam's story: when people feel that their boss truly cares about them, they will do and put up with almost anything to show their appreciation.

Second, you need to give your people Context. Make sure all employees know the *why* — the 'higher purpose' of the organisation, how each part of the organisation links to that purpose and why the daily actions of each individual matter — in other words, make sure each individual knows why what they do all day is important. Help people connect their personal values with the values of the organisation, thereby bringing personal meaning to their work. Remember the cathedral story? Remind them that they're 'serving God', rather than just laying bricks.

Third, provide Clarity: on what good looks like and what great looks like, both in terms of outcomes and behaviour. Many leaders assume people know what they need to do — and they're often wrong. Put the energy in upfront to make goals and expectations so clear that people can write their own performance review at the end of a period. Focus on a few key goals and remember to distinguish between lead and lag indicators to drive effective execution. Give continuous feedback on how people are going so that they can course correct. Remember the story about Chelvi's Big Hairy Audacious Goal (BHAG) to deliver one million new online customers in under a year? Use the power of stretch thinking to help individuals achieve more than they ever thought possible.

Fourth, remember to Clear the way: once people know what's expected of them, remember to ask what's in the way of them achieving it and then help clear those barriers out of the way. Remember that barriers come in many forms — from physical working conditions and resource gaps (remember the copy machine story?) to intellectual or training gaps. Be curious: go and look at how people are doing their job, since employees will sometimes take certain barriers for granted rather than complain about them. Help your people accelerate decision making, using the 'Session D' process (page 89) — don't be afraid to get into the detail from time to time. And don't neglect psychological barriers that people put up in their own minds — remember that most people are insecure and can be their own worst enemy when it comes to working effectively with others and achieving their potential.

Fifth, Celebrate! Make a habit of recognising people's success and contributions along the way. Use both formal and informal types of recognition frequently, and on regular big occasions. Remember that different individuals like to be recognised in different ways — some love public adulation, while others just want to feel like valued members of a loyal team — so use both top-down and bottom-up recognition. Make sure people know why they're being recognised, so that you reinforce a virtuous circle of performance. And be creative: remember the story of my early boss's letter to my parents? Find ways to cut through, with forms of recognition that show you really 'get' and care about the individual.

As a leader, ask yourself honestly whether you're actually doing all five of these things on a regular basis. If engagement scores are low, or you sense that some of your people are clearly demotivated, use the five points as the basis for re-setting the team's foundations.

And remember that *you* need to be authentic in your own purpose and intent if you want people to truly engage with your team — people can spot a phony a mile away. Do you really know your own purpose and values? How self-aware are you of your own motivations, strengths and weaknesses and emotional drivers? What steps are you taking to make sure you understand how others see you? And how empathetic are you — what effort are you making to understand how others see the world and to manage your own in-built biases? Remember to 'walk the floor' without an entourage, and be nice to the coffee person — they may save your bacon one day.

Finally, remember to work on the quality of your communications. None of the Leadership Star principles are going to be effective if you don't communicate well. Build an effective communications plan, use lots of different formal and informal channels to build an ongoing dialogue with your people and make sure you design messages (and stories) that stick — remember my family's trip to Disney World? Look for Simple, Unexpected, Concrete, Credible, Emotional Stories (SUCCES).

You don't have to be an extroverted public speaker to communicate effectively, but you also can't rely on your professional communications people to do it all for you. People need to hear your authentic voice, and you'll be a much more effective and engaging leader if you stay curious and engaged with people at all levels in your organisation.

A carefully designed plan based on the Leadership Star framework is fundamental to building long-term engagement, but sometimes you'll be faced with crisis situations that don't lend themselves to long-term engagement plans. In those situations, however, you'll typically find that one or two of the key points — usually Care, Context and Clarity — are the key to getting things back on track, with Clear the way and Celebrate as important follow-ons once the immediate issues are addressed.

Remember that people's needs are likely to shift during crisis, and different groups will see different concerns emerge. Communicating with empathy is essential to calm people down and keep them focused, while providing clarity through faster decision making and stretching goals can help avoid wheel-spinning and disengagement.

A final thought

Whether you're just starting out as a leader, or are already the CEO of a large organisation, I hope you've found the Leadership Star framework both a logical and compelling approach for you to use in building staff engagement.

For me, having the chance to lead a large organisation was incredibly personally fulfilling, despite the way it ended. It wasn't about personal achievement, the public attention or the financial rewards. Overwhelmingly, my satisfaction came from knowing that

I had helped a large number of people find meaning and personal satisfaction in their careers by contributing to something bigger than themselves. True leadership is about serving others. As scholar Clayton Christensen observed,

> *Management is the most noble of professions if it's practiced well. No other occupation offers as many ways to help others learn and grow, take responsibility and be recognized for achievement, and contribute to the success of a team.*

There is obviously a lot more to effective leadership of an organisation than staff engagement. There is even a lot more to effective human resource management itself than just staff engagement.

But I can't think of another single aspect of leadership that has a more direct impact on all the other disciplines, while providing the immense and enduring personal satisfaction that comes from helping others succeed.

So, get in there and start applying the five points of the Leadership Star. Just start. You don't have to get it all right from day one. You don't have to have a perfectly formed plan for each point in the star. Be disciplined, be authentic and ask your people for feedback as you go — don't be afraid to be vulnerable from time to time.

I can't promise it will take your organisation to global leadership or save your company from bankruptcy.

But I can promise that it will make you a better leader, make great people want to work with you, and create wonderful opportunities for both you and your people to prosper and grow.

Good luck!

THE LEADERSHIP
STAR: A SUMMARY

The following pages summarise the Leadership Star framework and the book's key points as a quick reference for readers.

Background

'Engagement' measures the extent to which an employee is psychologically committed to their organisation and the work that they are doing. Organisations typically calculate overall and business unit level engagement scores through staff surveys provided by firms such as Aon Hewitt or Gallup, enabling them to compare their results with those of other organisations.

Although many factors contribute to an organisation's success, statistical research demonstrates that organisations with high engagement tend to deliver better results across a range of financial, customer and employee measures. And while high engagement sometimes is itself the result of high performance, an organisation that consistently attracts and retains high performers — and provides an emotionally engaging environment in which they can thrive — is likely to outperform competitors over time.

Leaders who focus on building engagement among their people therefore increase the chances of building sustainable high performance—as well as giving them the personal satisfaction of knowing that they have been able to have a positive impact on other people's lives.

The Leadership Star framework

While 'macro' factors—industry dynamics, competitive position, external reputation, compensation structures, training programs, and so on—can affect an organisation's engagement score, actions by leaders at all levels play a critical role in how individual employees feel about their organisation and their role.

The Leadership Star—five key points, each starting with C—reminds leaders of the key actions they need to take to build and sustain engagement over time.

These five points are:

1. Care

2. Provide Context

3. Give Clarity

4. Clear the way

5. Celebrate.

1. Care

Genuine Care is the foundation of high engagement. Highly engaging leaders manifest that Care in several ways. They show they Care:

- for the individual as a human being: rather than treating people as collective 'human resources', great leaders strive to treat each person in their organisation as a valued individual. They also recognise that 'care' is an action word, by:
  - acknowledging their humanity: taking an interest in them as people and showing that they value each person for who they are, not just for what they do or their position in the hierarchy

- demonstrating empathy and compassion, offering emotional support during both work and personal challenges

- helping meet their individual needs or constraints, adjusting expectations when possible.

- about their development and growth: people want to feel that they are being challenged, that they are growing in skills and experience and that they have a bright future. Highly engaging leaders create a culture of development by:

  - understanding people's abilities and aspirations

  - giving honest feedback and advice

  - investing in their growth

  - investing in training and development resources

  - taking risks on people.

- about results: people need to know that their leaders are committed to excellence and delivering results. Leaders need to set high standards, offering encouragement where possible and delivering tough love where necessary. This is because success breeds success: a team that consistently achieves stretching goals is more likely to feel proud and confident in its capabilities, and as a consequence to become highly engaged.

2. Provide Context

Highly engaging leaders help people find meaning in what they do, by explaining the higher purpose of the organisation and helping people connect that purpose to their own values and daily work. To do this, engaging leaders:

- define and explain the organisation's purpose (in other words, the 'why' of the organisation): what outcomes does the organisation seek to deliver, and for whom?

- define and explain the organisation's priorities as it seeks to deliver on its purpose

- demonstrate their own personal commitment to that purpose and the organisation's priorities

- help people see how their individual roles link to and support the purpose and priorities, and ideally how their work aligns with their own personal values

- constantly communicate and reinforce the purpose and priorities, especially when making key decisions.

3. Give Clarity

To build and sustain engagement, leaders need to ensure people know what's expected of them, in several respects:

- *Role Clarity:* people need to understand the purpose of their individual role and how they are expected to contribute as a member of the team. Good leaders make a point of clarifying their expectations for each role in detail, so that people are more likely to spend their time on the right things and to work effectively with their colleagues to deliver high-quality results.

- *Goal Clarity:* for each performance period, individuals need to know what outcomes are expected — what 'good' looks like, and what 'great' looks like. Effective goal setting means choosing a small but impactful set of stretch objectives, clarifying the difference between lead and lag indicators and encouraging people to adopt a 'growth mindset' in their approach to meeting their objectives.

- *Behavioural Clarity:* in a highly engaged culture, everyone is clear on the organisation's values and understands how those values translate into what behaviour is expected and what behaviour isn't acceptable.

- *Regular feedback:* great leaders ensure that people get regular formal and informal feedback on both their performance and their behaviour, reinforcing good results and allowing people to course-correct where they're off track. Ideally that feedback allows people to understand both absolute performance — how they have performed against their goals — and relative performance — how their outcomes stack up in the broader organisation.

- *Consequences:* highly engaged organisations make sure that individuals are both recognised and held to account for their performance, whether in terms of goal delivery or behaviour. Where consequences relate to breaches of behavioural standards, it's important that these steps are sufficiently public that the organisation recognises the leader's commitment to their avowed standards.

4. Clear the way

Once people are clear on what's expected of them, leaders need to be proactive in helping knock down the barriers that hold people back. This means:

- asking what's getting in the way — physical constraints, financial or resource limitations, lack of knowledge, emotional or cultural barriers or political issues

- personally looking for barriers that employees may not see or recognise by talking to customers, suppliers and employees, and by digging into the details of processes

- taking action to remove those barriers, whether through direct decisions and resource allocation or by using techniques such as 'Session D' (see chapter 4) to quickly surface and resolve barriers to success.

5. Celebrate

The final step in sustaining engagement is to recognise individual contributions and success, creating a powerful feedback loop for performance and engagement. In highly engaged organisations, recognition is embedded as a fundamental aspect of the culture and operates at a number of levels:

- *Frequent and periodic:* leaders make a point of frequently recognising the value of day-to-day efforts, while also stepping back from time to time to celebrate major milestones such as the achievement of quarterly or annual results.

- *Top down and bottom up:* rather than using a purely senior leader–driven effort, highly engaged organisations use both peer and team-leader recognition programs to reinforce gratitude and pride among employees at all levels and strengthen the emotional bonds within and among teams.

- *Informal and formal:* while formal financial (such as, performance pay) and nonfinancial (such as, awards nights) recognition programs play an important part in recognition, the best leaders use a wide variety of informal approaches to create recognition that has emotional impact. From 'thank you' notes to gifts to new development opportunities, the range of approaches is limited only by the leader's creativity — so long as the recognition is delivered in a manner that is authentic, relevant and personalised to the individual in question.

- *Individual and team:* to maximise engagement, recognition programs need to celebrate team performance as well as individual achievement. In most organisations, there are many 'unsung heroes' whose roles may not allow them to stand out as individual achievers, but whose experience and efforts are nevertheless critical to the organisation's success.

- *Focused and fair:* who gets recognised — and for what — sends important messages to the organisation about what *really* matters to the leaders. Likewise, employees look closely at the signals embedded in recognition programs: the relative value provided for performance versus behaviour, and the actions that are taken (or not taken) on people who fall short.

Growing as a leader

The five steps of the Leadership Star provide a useful framework for leaders to build engagement. However, there are two other essential ingredients for leaders who want to sustain and grow that engagement over time: the character and behaviour of the leader, and how the leader communicates.

First, the character and behaviour of the leader themselves is critical. Highly engaging leaders stand out through the way they demonstrate:

- *Personal values and purpose:* the best leaders are clear about why they do what they do, the principles that they live their life by and how their leadership role aligns with that purpose and their principles and values.

- *Self-awareness:* the best leaders understand their own strengths, weaknesses and emotional drivers and become masterful at managing themselves accordingly. They also maintain a level of curiosity and humility that drives them to continually seek feedback and find ways to improve.

- *Empathy:* the most engaging leaders demonstrate a high level of empathy and emotional intelligence that allows them to connect with all sorts of people at all levels in the organisation. By role-modelling a commitment to transparency and admitting vulnerability, they create a 'safe' and trusting environment that sets a standard for leaders and employees throughout the organisation.

- *Energy:* leadership can be relentlessly challenging. By managing their energy carefully — through prioritising sleep, selectively switching off, finding their source of energy at work and having fun — they are able to set a strong and sustainable tone for the organisation that helps people overcome the inevitable challenges.

Second, focused, effective and ongoing communications are critical to embedding and reinforcing each aspect of the Leadership Star. In highly engaged organisations this is achieved by:

- *Building a structured communications plan:* this means identifying in advance the key stakeholder groups that need to be engaged, the key messages by month for that group (using the five points of the Leadership Star as a reference to ensure key topics are covered regularly) and the mechanism by which those messages will be communicated (for example, by email, town hall meeting, and so on.).

- *Using multiple channels to target the audience:* a range of venues (large and small meetings) and techniques (emails, floor-walks, videos) all have their place in communicating and reinforcing engagement messages. The best leaders use them all rather than relying on only one or two approaches (such as an all-staff email and quarterly town hall).

- *Designing messages that 'stick'*: using the Heath brothers' 'SUCCES' framework (Simple, Unexpected, Concrete, Credible, Emotional Stories),[1] leaders can create stories that increase the impact and 'stickiness' of their messages. These stories are far more engaging than the typical corporate-speak email message.

- *Listening, adjusting and keeping at it*: leaders don't have to be natural born presenters to be effective communicators. Many different styles can work — what matters most in building engagement is that leaders are authentic in their commitment to the organisation's purpose and priorities, and take actions to demonstrate their commitment to delivering on all five points of the Leadership Star.

The Leadership Star framework is not a comprehensive approach to organisational leadership. But for leaders who believe that engagement is important to their success — or for those who are struggling to diagnose and address weak engagement results — the 'five Cs' are a great foundation for building a highly engaged organisation.

---

[1] See page 164.

AFTERWORD

In November of 2019, after nearly five years as CEO of Westpac, I got fired.

One of our regulators, Australian Transaction Reports and Analysis Centre (AUSTRAC), announced that they were launching proceedings against us in the Federal Court for alleged breaches of anti-money laundering laws. Although much of what was in the allegations related to errors that my team had identified and reported to AUSTRAC over a year earlier, there were new, deeply upsetting allegations that we had failed to adequately monitor payments to the Philippines, some of which may have been used to fund child exploitation.

In the immediate aftermath of AUSTRAC's announcement (I'd been given a heads-up the night before that it was coming), I drove to the bank's financial crime operations centre in western Sydney. Standing in a common area, surrounded by several dozen shell-shocked members of the team, I explained what I knew about what had happened and tried to answer their questions as best I could. I then met in a conference room with the team leaders, who took me through the details of what they'd been able to glean from AUSTRAC's specific claims. Though they were devastated by the news, they remained calm and professional and explained their processes and cited examples in sufficient detail that I was able to take our board through the facts as I understood them that evening.

Through the following weekend I chaired meetings with our senior executives as we worked through the new allegations and developed our response. Everyone was deeply upset by these new allegations — I had previously chaired Save the Children in Australia, which made me particularly sensitive to the scourge of child exploitation, and horrified at the thought that we had somehow missed an opportunity to stop it.

Despite the shock and dismay among the senior team at these allegations, I couldn't have been prouder of how the team responded. There was no defensiveness, no animosity between units involved — just a relentless focus on getting to the bottom of what had happened, fixing the issue, and finding ways to demonstrate our genuine remorse by making something good come out of something bad.

All the work we had done as a team — on our core purpose of helping, our commitment to our values, and to demonstrating genuine care for each other and for our people — came to the fore. We couldn't control what was going on externally, but we could control how we responded. In the space of a few hours we developed a comprehensive plan to address the core issues, to work through the legal processes with our regulators, and, as a sign of our genuine remorse for what had happened, to make game-changing contributions to organisations that were fighting child exploitation in places such as the Philippines.

In the days that followed, a political and media storm erupted that smashed our stock price and did enormous damage to the company's reputation. Politicians, media commentators and regulators around the globe demanded explanations and accountability. Photographers staked out my house and reporters rang the doorbell seeking comment.

I understood that as the most senior executive I bore ultimate accountability for whatever happened in the company. Several large institutional shareholders and senior politicians called for my head, and the board and I agreed that, as the CEO, my position was untenable: I was out, and the chairman and chair of the Board Risk Committee announced that they would bring forward their retirement dates.

In the months that followed my departure, having spoken to former colleagues and read the various investigative reports on what happened, I've reflected on what went wrong and what I and my team could have done differently.

And while I'd love to have a time machine to go back and intervene so that these issues never happened, I accept that as a leader you may not control everything that happens on your watch, but you still own it.

It was hard to see the company I had been so proud to lead have its reputation dragged through the mud, especially since I loved and respected the people who worked there so much. At a personal level, it was disappointing to have my 30-year career in banking end in such a painfully abrupt way, when I had been trying so hard to be a force for good in leading the banking industry to a more sustainable and respected (by customers and the community) future.

There was, however, a bright spot that emerged, giving me great confidence that the company will overcome these issues and bounce back both stronger and wiser from the experience.

In the days after the announcement of my departure, I received an unexpected outpouring of support from staff — from both within Westpac and from previous organisations I'd worked for. Over 500 staff, many of whom I'd never met, sent personal notes via email. Many posted comments on Yammer (our internal social networking site) and a number of staff and former employees took to LinkedIn to express their support.

Some expressed gratitude for the way I'd led the company or committed to an initiative that they felt was important. Some thanked me for a personal comment or advice I'd given them along the way. Many talked about how proud they felt to work at Westpac, and how upset they were about how the company was being portrayed. And most satisfyingly, a large number reassured me how committed they remained to delivering great service and living the values of the organisation — two of the main themes I championed as CEO.

While the comments were notionally directed at me, what they really showed was how the individuals felt about the company and their co-workers: they were committed. Despite the disturbing accusations that were being made in the newspapers, the employees overwhelmingly remained engaged and committed to the purpose and values of the organisation.

That's not to say that the AUSTRAC actions, and the coronavirus pandemic that hit so shortly thereafter, haven't had a negative effect on engagement: it's inevitable that negative publicity and the ongoing impact of change will take its toll on morale.

It's also clear that the current board and management have a big job to do to restore the bank's reputation and rebuild morale — both in response to the regulatory issues and the human and economic challenges created by the COVID-19 crisis. This will inevitably require difficult decisions and an acceleration of changes to the way the bank is run.

But I'm confident that the fundamental commitment of leaders at all levels to live the five points of the Leadership Star means that Westpac will bounce back stronger than ever.

APPENDIX A
A BALANCED
APPROACH TO
PERFORMANCE
ASSESSMENT

The performance management process—and conducting performance reviews in particular—is often a source of frustration for leaders.

Theoretically, a good performance assessment process allows the leader to:

- measure an employee's performance against the goals they set

- provide feedback on what they're doing well and where they need to improve

- determine rewards—bonuses, salary increases, promotions, and so on.

- communicate rewards in a way that the employee will accept as fair.

In practice, both leaders and employees often find these processes hugely time-consuming, overly bureaucratic, and unsatisfying in the way they support development conversations and link performance and reward.

What follows is an approach I developed through trial and error over the years that works well in addressing these concerns. The output is a one-page, two-sided document that covers both target achievement and behaviour, and supports a content-rich development discussion between the employee and their leader.

The keys to this approach are to:

1. Set a small number of objective and subjective goals.

2. Have the employee conduct their own initial self-assessment.

3. Separate the rating and remuneration discussions.

1. Set a small number of objective and subjective goals

In a typical balanced scorecard approach to performance management, the leader sets out a number of different targets, each of which is assigned a weighting, that collectively add to 100 per cent. At the end of the year or performance period, the overall outcome for the employee is calculated as a weighted average (individual scores multiplied by the weighting factor for that score).

While logical, this approach to target setting can suffer from a number of challenges:

- too *few* measures, and important responsibilities are missed

- too *many* measures, and both employee and manager lose focus as the review process becomes a marathon exercise in document preparation and quibbling over the scores and weightings of relatively minor variables

- too *mechanistic*, and an over-reliance on numerically measurable targets can mean that there is little room for judgement or helpful development feedback.

So the first challenge is to pick a smallish number of goals, which includes a mix of measurable and subjective targets. For each of these targets, the leader and employee should agree on both 'good' and 'great' performance levels (see chapter 3 for a discussion on setting 'good' versus 'great' targets).

Picking the right number of goals

The right number of goals for each role depends on both its scope and the current business situation. In a steady-state, well-performing business, a narrow role in sales, service or operations might have three to four key performance areas, with two to three component metrics in each. Example measures could include:

- *sales:* specific revenue or volume growth across 2 to 3 major products

- *service:* customer satisfaction and retention scores

- *financial:* cost reduction and cash flow metrics

- *operational:* processing volume and quality/error rates

- *project delivery:* milestone completion and cost/benefit achievement

- *people management:* health and safety, staff turnover, engagement scores.

These measures should be clear and quantifiable, so that there is little room for debate about whether the 'good' or 'great' target has been achieved.

More senior or large people leadership roles will typically be measured across a broader range of five to six categories. In addition to macro-level measures in the categories just listed (for example, overall profitability or customer 'Net Promoter Scores'), such roles might be measured against more subjective areas such as:

- *strategic change:* for example, development of new business strategies; merger/acquisitions/partnership development; business reengineering and restructuring; new product development; technology investments

- *people leadership:* for example, talent acquisition/retention; training and development; industrial relations outcomes; staff engagement strategies; communication and whistleblowing system effectiveness; diversity and inclusion; employee wellbeing

- *risk management:* for example, improvement in risk/compliance outcomes; reduction in high risk/low return activities; reduced inventory shrinkage; contingency and business continuity planning

- *community engagement:* for example, reputation-building activities and partnerships; environmental performance; political/regulatory relationship management; sponsorship and brand effectiveness.

Where possible, these areas should seek to include quantifiable outcomes — new products launched, safety scores achieved, audit ratings improvements, and so on. At a minimum, however, leaders should clearly articulate the desired target state for both 'good' and 'great' performance.

Objective versus subjective measurement

To my mind, the measure of a good performance scorecard is that it is clear enough that the individual can largely perform their own review. The exception is the inclusion of a few subjective ratings that the leader determines.

For example, each of my direct reports invariably has a people leadership goal that reads 'Improve management bench strength' — with the specific target described as 'Leader to assess'. Another such measure is 'Demonstrate improved use of data-driven decision making'.

To assess these, I would ask the individual to explain to me what specific steps they had taken and show what outcomes had been achieved. Based on this explanation and evidence, I would then make a judgement as to whether this reflected 'expected', 'high' or 'below-par' performance in the circumstances.

The same approach applies to the behaviour assessment — as discussed in chapter 3, each employee's behaviour is rated against each of the organisation's values on an A ('role model'), B ('lives the values'), or C ('issues to discuss') scale.

In short, don't be afraid to *explicitly* embed judgement in your performance assessments. Judgement is always present when leaders think about employee performance — calling it out explicitly forces us to think carefully about the judgements we make, and articulating that judgement helps employees develop and grow.

The performance document

If you follow this approach, at the start of the performance period each employee has a single piece of paper comprised of two tables: on one side, their performance goals, and on the other side their behavioural standards.

For example, the first page might look like table A (overleaf).

Note that this page *doesn't* include everything that the individual is responsible for in their role description. Rather, these are the critical areas where the leader wants discretionary effort to be focused during the period. The employee is still on the hook for the items in their job description, but it is assumed that they will do these things. If gaps emerge — or significant outperformance is observed — that can be dealt with in the rating or ranking discussion, as explained in the next section.

The second page of the document focuses on behaviour, and is aligned to the organisation's values, as shown in table B (overleaf).

Table A: performance targets (for Period 202X)

Financial (25%)		Customer (25%)		Strategic Progress (25%)	
Good	Great	Good	Great	Good	Great
Return on capital:		*NPS:*		*Innovation:*	
>10%	>15%	5 point increase	10 point increase	Successful launch of premium product	Premium product captures 5% share
Sales:		*Error rates:*		*Project delivery:*	
5% increase	10% increase	5% drop in …	10% drop in …	Launch new digital platform	Complete migration to new platform, de-commission old platform
Profit:		*Complaints:*		*Data usage:*	
10% increase	18% increase	10% reduction	20% reduction	Demonstrate improved data driven-decisions	Leader to assess
Cost:		*Market share:*			
1% increase	5% reduction	1% increase in product X	3% increase in product X		

Risk Management (15%)		People Leadership (10%)		Comments:	
Good	Great	Good	Great		
Fraud losses:		*Safety:*			
Reduce by 10%	Reduce by 20%	10% LTIFR reduction	No LTIs		
Audit reports:		*Engagement:*			
Reduce rating 4s	No rating 4s	5 point increase	10 point increase		
Compliance:		*Leadership bench:*			
No breaches	Demonstrate significant control improvements	Improve bench strength	Leader to assess		
		Diversity:			
		Achieve female leadership target	Leader to assess		

Table B: behaviour assessment

Organisational Value	Description	Assessment (A/B/C)	Comment/ Examples
Integrity	Maintain high ethical standards. Meet commitments. Don't shade the truth. Have courageous conversations.	Role Model	
Service	Put customer's needs first. Deliver a great experience and look for ways to meet both expressed and unexpressed needs.	Lives the values	
Curiosity	Don't take current business for granted. Look for opportunities to innovate. Use data to understand and improve everything we do.	Lives the values	
Collaboration	Build strong relationships with your team and peers. Be generous with your time — look for ways to help others succeed.	Role Model	
Delivery	Overcome obstacles and find a way to get things done. Deliver great results for both customers and shareholders.	Role Model	
Overall Assessment:		*Role Model*	

2. Have the employee conduct their own initial self-assessment

From a development perspective, I believe it's important to have the employee complete their own draft performance assessment. This is because it helps them take ownership of their results — whether good, great or below par — and helps boost their self-awareness as they consider how their boss will assess the judgemental components of their review.

On page one, this should be relatively straightforward as they simply mark or circle the actual performance result against each target (assuming the data is available). For judgemental areas, they need to identify what evidence they can provide to justify their rating.

On page two, I ask employees to rate themselves A ('role model'), B ('lives the values'), or C ('issues to discuss') against each of the organisation's values, and to note examples to justify their rating. While some people find it challenging to assess themselves as either 'role models' or having 'issues', the process forces them to think about their behaviour and what examples they — and their leader — can use to justify their assessment.

For both the performance and the behaviour pages, this process of self-evaluation against relatively objective standards helps reinforce self-awareness and puts the employee in a better frame of mind for the subsequent performance discussions with their leader.

3. Separate the rating and remuneration discussions

Having two separate conversations — one to discuss performance against the agreed standards, and the second to discuss remuneration outcomes — is critical to making both conversations constructive.

When the two conversations are the same — 'Here's your performance rating, and here's the bonus/raise you're getting as a result' — the employee's focus naturally tends to be on the second part of the conversation, and they'll feel relatively good or bad depending on the result.

In addition, combining the two conversations means that leaders often feel the need to reverse-engineer the performance rating in order to justify the financial outcomes that the employee is going to receive. This can often lead to the conversation devolving into arguments about specific targets and whether or not the remuneration outcomes are 'fair' given what was achieved against the targets.

In my approach, the first conversation — what I call the 'rating' conversation — focuses exclusively on performance against the goals and standards that were set at the start of the period.

You may want to *start* the rating discussion with the behaviour page, since this helps reinforce that values and behaviour are taken seriously — values are made manifest by behaviour, and focusing on this page shows that you expect your leaders to be role models for the values.

On the performance page, the discussion is along the lines of 'I asked you to do X, and you achieved it'. You acknowledge and praise the employee for what was achieved against the targets and provide your perspective on areas where the employee fell short or needs to improve. This helps the employee feel acknowledged and proud of what they've achieved, and to be more open-minded and accepting of constructive feedback.

For judgemental areas, I will typically ask the employee to explain what rating they think they should get, and then use differences between their assessment and my judgement as the basis for a constructive development conversation. It's important that this is a two-way conversation, and the employee's perspectives on what they did well and where they could have done better is important input to an ultimate judgement on pay and promotions.

In the second conversation, the task is to explain remuneration outcomes in the context of *relative* performance. In this framework, the performance rating is an input, but the ultimate outcome needs to be adjusted based on the leader's judgement about:

- degree of difficulty in hitting the targets

- relative performance of others in the team

- relative value of the individual's contribution to the overall result

- changes in market conditions during the period (that is, headwinds and tailwinds)

- changes in business priorities during the period

- incremental value delivered beyond the scope of the performance document

- appropriate consequences for negative behaviour, risk or compliance incidents.

This conversation is typically along the lines of:

In our last conversation we talked about how your performance rating was strong versus the targets that we set. In thinking about the right pay outcomes this year, I have recognised that you were without half your team for three months but also that the drop in our supply prices gave your division a big head start on margins. Plus, the middle market division had a particularly strong six months. Also, in my judgement you haven't done as much as you promised you would do to fix the relationship issues between your team and operations. So, on balance your outcome is a bit lower than it otherwise would have been ...

While the employee may still not be satisfied with the outcome, being explicit about how they performed against their targets, and the various factors that play into your judgement on pay and promotions, helps people save face and appreciate the fairness with which you are approaching the issue.

If you find performance reviews frustrating, I highly recommend trying this two-step approach: it turns the performance conversation from an adversarial one into a more constructive, development-oriented conversation, thereby reinforcing your commitment to them and their personal growth.

APPENDIX B
COMMUNICATION
CHANNEL DO'S
AND DON'TS

Chapter 7 includes a summary of the various communication channels you can use to get your engagement messages out, and some of the key success factors for each of them.

What follows is a more detailed explanation of each channel, and the best practices for each that I've picked up over the years.

Large group presentations and conferences

There are several advantages of large group presentations: they're efficient, since many people hear the same messages at once. In the hands of a skilled presenter, they can generate demonstrable enthusiasm that creates 'social proof' for those who might otherwise be on the fence. And, if stage-managed well, they can reinforce a sense of 'occasion' that breaks through complacency and builds engagement among the participants.

Large events aren't without risk. Even for experienced presenters, speaking without a script can lead to slips of the tongue or poor word choices that get taken the wrong way. Nervous energy in a more 'staged' setting can lead people to misinterpret your motives or intentions. And if you or the presenters come off as inauthentic, out of touch, arrogant, muddled or lacking energy, then you can quickly *dis*engage a large group of people.

As with any presentation, to minimise this risk:

- *Prepare carefully.* It's obvious, but don't delegate an important presentation to the communications team and think you can fix it up the day before. Start planning weeks, if not months, in advance and meet regularly to review progress — it will help shape your own thinking and enthusiasm.

- *Rehearse.* Steve Jobs used to rehearse his famous product launches for hours on end. The more you rehearse, the more your brain can focus on the nuances of your presentation rather than trying to remember what comes next.

- *Use 'fold back' screens.* I prefer to use two large flat-panel screens on the floor, with one showing my speaking notes and the other showing the current slide on the screen. Teleprompters can also be helpful, but require practice to avoid looking too formal and scripted — you want to connect with your audience, and unless you are very skilled, reading a script quickly forms an invisible barrier to emotional connection. If you don't have access to this sort of technology, then a printed table of three columns — listing slide headings, key points for each and transition statements — can do the trick.

- *Avoid death by PowerPoint.* Simple graphics are best. Too many slides and unreadable graphics or text destroy any emotional connection to the presenter. Remember that YOU are the presentation, not your slides.

- *Involve the audience.* When trying to build engagement, make sure you break the ice at the beginning to put people in an open and receptive mood. One executive I know regularly asked everyone to stand up and hug their neighbour. Amusing 'call and response' chants can work as well. During the presentation itself, build in breaks where you ask the audience to talk to their neighbour about an issue you've raised and then to write down their thoughts. Consider calling on members of the audience and using roving microphones to elicit comments and questions. All of these techniques help drag 'spectators' into the session emotionally.

• *Celebrate the locals.* If you are quite senior or unfamiliar to your audience, you may face scepticism or cynicism about anything you say. Involving representative staff members who are either part of or known to the audience — as MCs, Q&A moderators, panellists or presenters — helps build credibility and buy-in.

• *Don't neglect the 'wow' factor.* While too much 'Hollywood' can overwhelm the message, it's important that people see formal presentations as something memorable and important. It doesn't have to be expensive, but staging, lighting, catchy entry music, costumes and dress codes; technology demonstrations and videos; live performances, surprise guests, humorous gags, food and drinks, and even symbolic gifts can help the session stand out and leave the audience with a stronger connection to you and the organisation.

Communication workshops and cascade meetings

One effective way to kick off a new or renewed focus on staff engagement is to conduct a series of workshops that cascade through the organisation, ultimately including everyone.

Typically, these start with an offsite workshop among the top team to agree on the key messages — mission/purpose, values, goals — and the language and stories to be used to communicate them to the broader organisation.

Once these have been clarified, a series of cascading workshops are conducted, with each member of the top team leading a workshop with their team, and so on through the organisation. These workshops typically follow a scripted agenda—prepared by the communications or HR team—that provides the meeting facilitator with key messages and scenarios for the groups to work through. The goal of these sessions, aside from explaining the key messages, is to generate stories that help each participant connect the organisation's messages to their own personal values, goals and role.

As with formal presentations, bringing large numbers of people together in a single venue to conduct these sessions can bring a sense of occasion to the messages that further reinforces the importance and connection that people feel for the messages themselves.

Smaller town hall meetings

Smaller format meetings of say, 20 to 100 people are a great way to build engagement. If held in the team's own environment—in a large conference room, cafeteria or even as a stand-up in an open-plan office—they create a sense of intimacy and informality that means people tend to be more engaged and open to both listening and giving feedback.

While a short formal presentation—a few key points backed up by five to ten slides, if any—can be a useful way to communicate key messages, the best value comes from creating the sense that this is just a large group conversation.

Sit-down interviews or panel sessions work well in this environment, with a few scripted questions to kick things off opening up to broader audience participation. One caution though—having more than two or three people on a panel usually degenerates into a series of scripted statements rather than an engaging conversation.

In these environments, it's not so much what you say as how you say it—and the impression you create—that drives engagement. Most people instinctively want to buy into their leader, and if they see that leader as authentic, open, thoughtful, empathetic, honest and even vulnerable, that goes a long way to building trust and engagement. You don't have to have all the answers—sometimes admitting you don't know, or turning the question around on the questioner, is a great way to draw out insights that people might not otherwise share on how you can clear the way for them. Just be careful not to be too flippant or disdainful in your answers — a cutting remark in public from one's boss is a wound that heals very slowly, if at all.

Team visits and floor-walks

Informal team visits and floor-walks are another great way to build connections with people, but they too need to be handled carefully.

When done well, informal visits and floor-walks humanise you as a leader, show people that you care and give you unfiltered learning about what's really going on.

The challenge with these visits is to avoid them being so scripted that people are more relieved when you've left than they are excited when you arrive.

In their (understandable) desire to have senior visits go well, local leaders or organisers can cause these visits to take on the air of a royal visit to a fertiliser factory, with rows of people in a receiving line, mumbling platitudes. Rather, try to keep these visits as low-key as possible: taking the time to greet people by name and show a genuine interest in their work and issues can go a long way.

Prepare in advance by getting the names (and photographs, if possible) of the people you're going to meet, so you can greet them by name and ask after people who are missing. Review key facts and statistics about the area's performance and current priorities so you can show that their work matters. And ask to see the 'back of house' areas — team rooms, cafeterias, filing and computer rooms, stationery cupboards, and so on: it's a great way to get a sense of what daily life is really like for your people, as well as to show your genuine interest in people and their welfare.

Project/business reviews

Project and business review meetings — while ostensibly focused on operational performance and delivery — can also serve to build or hurt engagement. The Session D approach described in chapter 4 is one example of how to do this well; reviews give leaders the chance to reinforce why a particular project or team is important and explain how the work relates to the organisation's context.

The main thing to be careful of is how criticism is delivered: in their desire to look 'tough' or 'smart', many leaders (myself occasionally included) fall into the trap of criticising the presenting team in ways that undermine their confidence and commitment — succeeding only in demotivating both the project team and everyone else who witnesses the bollocking.

Short, prepared presentations by people in the business can be an efficient way to learn and get feedback, as well as build pride among the people you're visiting. But be careful to set clear guidelines in advance that leave enough time for discussion and questions. If you're the visiting leader, chances are that people will see this as their big chance to shine, and their presentations will almost inevitably run over time.

Skip-level meetings

Skip-level meetings are another useful communication method. This is simply a round-table discussion with all the members of a team, without their boss (one of your direct reports) present.

While I will typically ask for feedback on their boss at the end of the meeting, the main purpose is to give people the chance to:

- connect directly with you and your priorities

- update you on their priorities

- be recognised by you for what is going well

- raise any issues or concerns they would otherwise avoid if their boss were present.

Informal coffees/lunches

In a large organisation, it can be challenging to create personal connections through different levels, departments and locations. Large presentations and town hall meetings help, but don't typically create the intimacy of a small group discussion.

One solution is to organise informal lunches or coffee catch-ups with a sampling of people from different parts of the organisation. These might include a selection of recent hires, high-potential junior people, female leaders, high-performing salespeople, or known 'influencers' who all work in a particular location.

Held in an informal setting, with low-key food and/or drinks to help put people at ease, a group of six to ten people can engage more deeply and authentically with you around the organisation's context and priorities, as well as sharing their observations on what's working and what isn't (thereby helping you to identify areas where you can clear the way).

When these meetings are managed well, people return to their teams as advocates for you and the organisation's agenda, thereby creating a network of people throughout the organisation who will vouch for your authenticity and commitment (as well as serving as useful contacts in the future when you need to take the pulse on an issue).

Larger drinks parties or lunches can serve a similar purpose, but in my experience the need to get around a larger group makes the engagement value somewhat limited — unless it is as part of a formal recognition function, as discussed in chapter 5.

One-on-one communications

Another way to build a network of highly engaged advocates is through direct communications with individual staff members — typically prompted by recognition of a particular achievement, contribution, career milestone or life event (new baby, buying a home, family illness, and so on).

Hand-written cards, emails, personal phone calls or even a surprise visit can create a huge impression, reinforcing both Care and Celebration. Individual contacts don't need to take a huge amount of time — in my experience people are usually so pleased and embarrassed that they want to get off the phone relatively quickly. But by scheduling time for these contacts each month, you can quickly build up a significant number of people who feel valued and engaged, and proudly share their experience with their colleagues.

For example, each month at Westpac I used to personally sign around 100 career anniversary certificates (for people achieving more than 20 years of service) and would make personal calls to people reaching 40, 45 and 50-year service milestones. I could have had the signatures printed (or even forged), but felt that the hour or so I spent on this each month was time well spent, since it meant that over 1000 people a year — spread across the entire organisation — received something that they knew came directly from the leader of their organisation.

The advent of phones with high-quality video recording means leaders can now send personalised congratulations to teams who achieve something important, or to well-regarded staff who are retiring. By personalising the leader's message and linking achievements to the organisation's purpose and priorities, these videos create a 'magic moment' for the individual or team that also reinforces the leader's Care, Context and commitment to Celebration for everyone watching.

Offering to mentor high-potential staff — or simply letting them shadow you for a day — is another way to communicate through action. Direct discussions let you reinforce your values and expectations, which the individual will share with their colleagues, while others who see you with a shadow will clock your commitment to developing people.

Electronic communications

Modern technology gives leaders a myriad ways to connect with their broader teams and reinforce engagement messages and dialogue.

All-staff emails, intranet blogs, webchats, collaboration tools such as Slack and Microsoft Teams, as well as internal social media applications such as Yammer and Workplace from Facebook, have revolutionised two-way communication with staff.

At Westpac we introduced Yammer on my first day as CEO, and it became a major enabler of collaboration and engagement. For the first time, any staff member could find and interact with any other staff member—a bank manager in Western Australia, for example, could request help on a customer issue and get an instant response from several managers in other parts of the country. Meanwhile, every staff member could contact me directly and receive a public or private message straight back.

Some leaders may fear that this explosion of communication channels will overwhelm their ability to get any work done, but my experience was that with rare exceptions people were respectful of my time and didn't abuse the opportunity.

If you are fortunate enough to have a dedicated communications team, these channels can play a large and important role—with regular messages and interactions targeted to particular groups and communities of interest on the platform.

The most important tip I can give around these platforms is to make sure that anything posted under your name *sounds like you*. If your posts sound like you swallowed a corporate buzzword dictionary, people will quickly see them for what they are and switch off—with substantial damage to your reputation as an authentic leader and a missed opportunity for engaging your staff.

'Wallpaper'

Another idea is to use visual cues in the working environment to reinforce engagement messages. Large banners in office lobbies, elevator door surrounds, removable stickers on the inside of elevator doors, wall posters, mouse pads, screen savers, t-shirts and hats, and even 'branded' coffee cups and sleeves can create subtle but frequent reminders around the organisation's values, care for people, mission or goals—as well as reinforcing specific behaviours, such as 'speaking up', that are seen as critical to supporting the desired culture.

Wherever possible, use real staff, customers, suppliers, and so on, in both the visual aspects of the communication and in the supply of the material. This helps employees identify with the messages and minimises the chances of upsetting an existing customer or supplier who sees the work.

While too many slogans can make employees feel like they've been transported to a North Korean rally, surrounding people with consistent messages — and varying them a bit to keep them fresh over time — helps sustain the ideas and build buy-in once the enthusiasm generated by the big event has faded.

It's also worth building an element of surprise into these messages — changing the look overnight, for example, or having senior leaders in the lobby to greet people on their way in.

External communications and social media

So far, I've focused on the various internal communication channels by which leaders can build engagement. But *external* communications can also have a big *internal* impact.

Employees are often interested followers of media coverage on their organisation, taking pride when they receive favourable coverage (and feeling deflated when the coverage is negative). So it's worth remembering that, when participating in media or investor interviews, your comments will be seen by your own staff as much as by your customers, investors or the public.

Social media provides another opportunity for leaders to get their messages out to staff as well as the public. I personally found LinkedIn the most effective external channel to reach and engage staff, thanks to its professional orientation and the ability of individual staff members to comment and repost my messages to their own networks (thereby demonstrating and reinforcing their pride in the organisation).

In a similar vein, don't discount the role that advertising plays in people's perception of their own organisation. While ostensibly focused on customers, the external presentation of a company influences the employees' perceptions as well — since they are even more likely to notice and reflect on the style and messaging of ads, be they television, radio, print, outdoor billboards or digital.

I encourage senior business and HR leaders to keep a close eye on any external advertising to make sure it aligns well with internal messaging on purpose, values and priorities. Too many leaders entirely delegate advertising strategy and execution to their marketing department and external agencies, only to wake up to an enraged workforce when a 'clever' ad campaign inadvertently manages to ridicule them or something they hold dear.

Likewise, external advertising can be a great way to reinforce an important message to your people — since external advertising commitments are seen by employees as a sign that leaders 'must be serious'.

During my time in the UK, we had great success in lifting pride and engagement, not to mention service quality, through a 'recruitment' ad campaign. In posters placed all over the city's Underground network, the bank described the sort of people it was looking to hire as those who 'helped the old lady cross the street, helped the young mother get her pram up the escalator, and picked up the little girl's glove'. The ad generated around 100 new hires; but more importantly, it lifted the pride and engagement of several thousand staff who saw these ads on their way to and from work each day.

BIBLIOGRAPHY

Aon Human Capital. (n.d.). 'Employee Engagement'. Retrieved from https://www.aonhumancapital.com.au/Home/For-Employers/People-and-performance/Employee-engagement

Campbell, R. (11 September 2018). 'Why leaders should put people ahead of outcomes (if they really want to succeed)'. *Australian Financial Review.*

Carbonara, S. (2012). *Manager's Guide to Employee Engagement* (Briefcase Books). New York: McGraw-Hill Education.

Carreyrou, J. (2018). *Bad Blood: Secrets and Lies in a Silicon Valley Startup.* New York: Knopf Publishing Group.

Clinton, B. (July–August 2007). 'I See You'. Retrieved from https://www.harvardmagazine.com/2007/07/i-see-you.html

Collins, J. (2001). *Good to Great: Why Some Companies Make the Leap and Others Don't.* New York: Harper Business.

Coyle, D. (2018). *The Culture Code: The Secrets of Highly Successful Groups.* New York: Bantam Books.

Dignan, A. (2014). *Game Frame: Using Games as a Strategy for Success.* New York: Free Press.

Dweck, C. (2014). 'The Power of Believing that You Can Improve'. Retrieved from https://www.ted.com/talks/carol_dweck_the_power_of_believing_that_you_can_improve?language=en

Eurich, T. (4 January 2018). 'What Self-Awareness Really Is (and How to Cultivate It)'. Retrieved from https://hbr.org/2018/01/what-self-awareness-really-is-and-how-to-cultivate-it

Gallup. (n.d.). 'Engage Your Employees to See High Performance and Innovation'. Retrieved from https://www.gallup.com/workplace/229424/employee-engagement.aspx

Goodwin, D. K. (2018). *Leadership in Turbulent Times*. New York: Simon & Schuster.

Greenleaf, R. K. (2002). *Servant Leadership: A Journey into the Nature of Legitimate Power and Greatness*. Mahwah NJ: Paulist Press.

Harvard Business Review Staff. (2014). 'How Companies Can Profit from a "Growth Mindset"'. Retrieved from https://hbr.org/2014/11/how-companies-can-profit-from-a-growth-mindset

Harvard Health Publishing. (n.d.). 'Giving Thanks Can Make You Happier'. Retrieved from https://www.health.harvard.edu/healthbeat/giving-thanks-can-make-you-happier

Harvard Health Publishing. (5 June 2019). 'In Praise of Gratitude'. Retrieved from https://www.health.harvard.edu/mind-and-mood/in-praise-of-gratitude

Heath, C. & Heath, D. (2007). *Made to Stick : Why Some Ideas Survive and Others Die*. New York: Random House.

Hoffman, B. (14 July 2015). '5 Pitfalls to Understanding People's Motives'. Retrieved from https://www.elsevier.com/connect/5-pitfalls-to-understanding-peoples-motives

Jones, K. (30 January 2020). 'Ranked: The Most Valuable Brands in the World'. Retrieved from https://www.visualcapitalist.com/ranked-the-most-valuable-brands-in-the-world/

Kahneman, D. (2011). *Thinking, Fast and Slow*. New York: Farrar, Straus and Giroux.

Kakkar, H. & Sivanathan, N. (11 August 2017). *Why We Prefer Dominant Leaders in Uncertain Times*. Retrieved from https://hbr.org/2017/08/why-we-prefer-dominant-leaders-in-uncertain-times

Kennedy, J. F. (1961). *Address to Joint Session of Congress May 25, 1961*. Retrieved from https://www.jfklibrary.org/learn/about-jfk/historic-speeches/address-to-joint-session-of-congress-may-25-1961

Kolowich Cox, L. (n.d.). '17 Truly Inspiring Company Vision and Mission Statement Examples'. Retrieved from https://blog.hubspot.com/marketing/inspiring-company-mission-statements

Kotter, J. P. & Heskett, J. L. (2011). *Corporate Culture and Performance*. New York: Free Press.

Kouzes, J. M. & Posner, B. (2015). *Extraordinary Leadership in Australia & New Zealand: The Five Practices that Create Great Workplaces*. Milton, Qld: John Wiley & Sons Australia Ltd.

Kruse, K. (2012). *Employee Engagement 2.0: How to Motivate Your Team for High Performance*. CreateSpace Independent Publishing Platform.

Lencioni, P. (2015). *The Truth About Employee Engagement: A Fable About Addressing the Three Root Causes of Job Misery*. New York: John Wiley & Sons.

Mann, A. & Dvorak, N. (28 June 2016). 'Employee Recognition: Low Cost, High Impact'. Retrieved from https://www.gallup.com/workplace/236441/employee-recognition-low-cost-high-impact.aspx

Marciano, P. L. (2010). *Carrots and Sticks Don't Work: Build a Culture of Employee Engagement with the Principles of Respect*. New York: McGraw-Hill Education.

McChesney, C., Covey, S. & Huling, J. (2012). *The 4 Disciplines of Execution: Achieving Your Wildly Important Goals*. New York: Free Press.

McKinney, M. (13 January 2009). 'The Block of Wood That Became the First Sony Walkman'. Retrieved from https://www.leadershipnow.com/leadingblog/2009/01/the_block_of_wood_that_became.html

Missionstatements.com. (n.d.). 'Fortune 500 Mission Statements'. Retrieved from https://www.missionstatements.com/fortune_500_mission_statements.html

Morgan, B. (1 June 2020). '5 Customer Experience Lessons from USAA'. Retrieved from https://www.forbes.com/sites/blakemorgan/2020/06/01/5-customer-experience-lessons-from-usaa/#43f433ff7e54

Myers, C. (30 August 2016). 'The New "Rules of The Game": Balancing Profits And Social Responsibility In The 21st Century'. Retrieved from https://www.forbes.com/sites/chrismyers/2016/08/30/the-new-rules-of-the-game-balancing-profits-and-social-responsibility-in-the-21st-century/

Ranton, R. (2020). *Dauntless: Leadership Lessons from the Front Line.* Brisbane: Change Empire Books.

Reutskaja, E. L. et al. (1 October 2018). 'Choice Overload Reduces Neural Signatures Of Choice Set Value In Dorsal Striatum And Anterior Cingulate Cortex'. *Natural Human Behaviour 2*, pp. 925–935.

Rogers, P. & Blenko, M. W. (January 2006). 'Who Has the D?: How Clear Decision Roles Enhance Organizational Performance'. Retrieved from https://hbr.org/2006/01/who-has-the-d-how-clear-decision-roles-enhance-organizational-performance

Sinek, S. (2009). 'How Great Leaders Inspire Action'. Retrieved from https://www.ted.com/talks/simon_sinek_how_great_leaders_inspire_action

Sinek, S. (2009). *Start With Why: How Great Leaders Inspire Everyone to Take Action.* New York: Portfolio Penguin.

Smart, B. D. (2012). *Topgrading* (3rd ed.). New York: Portfolio.

Sorenson, S. (n.d.). 'How Employee Engagement Drives Growth'. Retrieved from https://www.gallup.com/workplace/236927/employee-engagement-drives-growth.aspx

UXM. (6 June 2011). 'Say It with a Word Cloud'. Retrieved from http://www.uxforthemasses.com/word-clouds/

Wong, J. & Brown, J. (6 June 2017). *How Gratitude Changes You and Your Brain.* Retrieved from https://greatergood.berkeley.edu/article/item/how_gratitude_changes_you_and_your_brain

Zetlin, M. (n.d.). 'The 9 Worst Mission Statements of All Time'. Retrieved from https://www.inc.com/minda-zetlin/9-worst-mission-statements-all-time.html

ABOUT THE AUTHOR

Brian Hartzer is an experienced executive, leadership mentor and investor who served as CEO of the Westpac Banking Group from 2015 to 2019.

Prior to his time as Westpac's CEO, Brian spent 15 years in senior executive roles at major banks in Australia and the UK. These roles included CEO at Westpac and divisional chief executive roles at the Royal Bank of Scotland Group and ANZ Banking Group. He has also served as Chairman of the Australian Banking Association and of the Retail Banking Committee of the British Bankers Association.

Prior to joining ANZ, Brian spent ten years as a financial services strategy consultant at First Manhattan Consulting Group in New York, Melbourne and San Francisco.

Outside of banking, he is a senior advisor to Quantium, a Sydney-based Data Science company, and serves as Chairman of the Australian Museum Foundation Trust as well as a Trustee of the Australian Museum. He has previously served as Chairman of Save the Children Australia, Director of the Financial Markets Foundation for Children and Chair of the Business Advisory Committee of the Australian National University.

He graduated with a degree in European History from Princeton University and is a Chartered Financial Analyst.

Brian holds dual US and Australian citizenship and lives in Sydney.

INDEX